ENDORSEMENTS

Larry's passion for the delivery of exceptional hospitality is evident throughout this inspirational and entertaining book. His expertise, born of real-world experience with some of the most revered brands in the business, rewards readers with practical examples of "dos and don'ts" that are definitely worth sharing. *The Spirit of Hospitality* is a must-read for practitioners who want to sharpen their service game … or motivate their staff to deliver this "spirit" every day.

    – **PETER C. YESAWICH**, PhD, Vice Chairman, Emeritus MMGY Global

Clearly and convincingly, Larry provides encouragement and inspiration, motivating his readers with profound simplicity and truth.

    – **ROBERTO E. WIRTH**, President and Managing Director, Hassler Roma

Within the pages of *The Spirit of Hospitality*, Larry Stuart pours out his wisdom in such a clear and inviting way that this book should find its way into the hands of every business leader who desires to build a great business. The book is chock full of practical advice and easy-to-grasp principles.

    – **DR. HOWARD EDINGTON**, Long-Time Senior Pastor of
First Presbyterian Church of Orlando

We have never been more competitive, delivering unique guest experiences from every nuance and brand imaginable. It's easy to forget the subtleties and frosting on the cake of life if we don't have the basics ingredients and recipes correct. This easy-read page turner should be required reading for anyone considering entering the provision of guest service experiences.

    – **JOHN BERNDT**, Emeritus President, Cipriani Hotels; VP, Marco Polo
Hotels; SVP Operations F&B, Caesars; GM, Ritz Carlton

In *The Spirit of Hospitality*, Larry takes readers on a unique journey into the world of hospitality. This is a must-read primer for anyone who is searching for proven guidelines to improve standards of service. I'm convinced this book will change—in a positive way—how to enhance guest service. The spirit instilled in this book is alive. Read it, and read again. It will be your compass!

— **LUCIO ARANCIBIA**, CEC–AAC; Emeritus Executive Chef, Excalibur Hotel & Casino; VP of F&B, Motor City Hotel & Casino

Reading Larry's book, *The Spirit of Hospitality*, took me back to the opening of the Walt Disney World Dolphin, where Larry developed and honed much of his philosophy on service. He, along with his teammates, helped make a culture that swept up our staff and managers alike and created an atmosphere unlike any I have experienced since. The Spirit of Hospitality will enthrall you with the possibilities and instill not only the importance of the basics, but the value of reinventing and stretching every day.

— **MICHAEL D. WELLY**, Emeritus General Manager, Walt Disney World Dolphin; President, Cairn Hospitality and Wellness Consulting

The Spirit of Hospitality is a culmination of a lifetime of hospitality. The successful team approaches and long-term winning formulas are applicable across a wide range of industries. This book serves as the gold standard for customer service.

— **ROBERT B SHAPIRO**, Financial Expert, CPA, ABV, PA

The Spirit of Hospitality reflects the extensive experience, passion, and generosity of its author. Larry Stuart has masterfully highlighted the benefits of creating a culture of genuine hospitality, which can, if internalized, reap tremendous individual and collective rewards. As a compendium of life-long examples, this work reveals a treasure trove of proven theories and common-sense practices. It is truly an indispensable read for every culinary/hospitality student, as well as for seasoned restaurant and foodservice professionals.

— **FERDINAND METZ**, President Emeritus, The Culinary Institute of America

Larry has written a wonderful and inspiring book based on a wealth of real life endeavors "on the line" and totally committed every time. His hard-earned wisdom and great insight are invaluable to those of us who share this passion.

    – **BOB REPPIN**, Director of Operations, Westin Lake Las Vegas Resort & Spa; Emeritus F&B Director, World Disney World Dolphin

When I'm around Larry Stuart, there is a confidence that more people need to have in this dark world. Not only does he have confidence in believing that others can be better, he also has a servant's heart.

    – **PASTOR HERKIE WALLS**, Former NFL player, Houston Oilers & Tampa Bay Buccaneers

In *The Spirit of Hospitality*, Larry Stuart has done a masterful job of introducing the sometimes-complicated aspects of creating a memorable "guest experience" in a way that both the veteran and the student will be well served by immersing themselves in the wisdom contained in its pages.

    – **JOHN R. LABRUZZO**, CHA Hospitality Expert; Emeritus VP, Tampa Hard Rock & Casino and VP, Tishman Hotel Corporation

A must-read for every business owner, CEO, hotel or restaurant owner, pastor, or anyone whose career is dependent on working with the public. Larry Stuart really proves that hospitality is not the fluff you put on top of what you're doing, but a mainstay part of your culture. This book is a real eye opener.

    – **DANIEL NEEDHAM**, ChFC; Past President, New England Financial Services

I can honestly say that over my 35+ years of hospitality experience, I have never met an individual more passionate and enthusiastic in our field than Larry Stuart. I promise you that not only will you enjoy reading *The Spirit of Hospitality*, but following his direction will have a pronounced impact on you and your organization.

    – **ERIC ROSENBAUM**, Emeritus VP, Sierra Lodging, Inc.

In all my 35-plus years as a practitioner & corporate customer service officer in the commercial aviation & ground transportation fields, I have never run across a more comprehensive and universal publication as *The Spirit of Hospitality*. From entry level to top leadership, I recommend Larry Stuart's book as a must-have for your library, as it's great for baseline training & use as a strategic planning tool in the art of customer service principles.

— **RON E. BRENNAN**, Commercial Aviation Executive

Whether setting a table with china and silver, crystal and linens, or paper plates and plastic flatware, the deliciousness of breaking bread and sharing the wine with others is a gift we must not ever lose. Through *The Spirit of Hospitality*, Larry Stuart is keeping the candle's flame lit!

— **JAMES W. UNDERWOOD**, Retired Rear Admiral, US Coast Guard

For many years, I've both witnessed and received Larry's hospitality as he has weaved it into his leadership skills. This book is a direct reflection of the practical tools that Larry uses in his own life and that you can easily implement into yours in order to instantly empower the spirit of hospitality that's hidden within us all.

— **DOCTOR DAVID UTH**, Senior Pastor of First Baptist Orlando

The Spirit of Hospitality

THE
SPIRIT
OF
HOSPITALITY

HOW TO ADD THE MISSING INGREDIENTS
YOUR BUSINESS NEEDS

LARRY STUART

NEW YORK

LONDON • NASHVILLE • MELBOURNE • VANCOUVER

The Spirit of Hospitality

How to Add the Missing Ingredients Your Business Needs

Published in New York, New York, by Morgan James Publishing. Morgan James is a trademark of Morgan James, LLC. www.MorganJamesPublishing.com

The Morgan James Speakers Group can bring authors to your live event. For more information or to book an event visit The Morgan James Speakers Group at www.TheMorganJamesSpeakersGroup.com.

ISBN 9781683509899 paperback
ISBN 9781683509905 eBook
Library of Congress Control Number: 2018934767

Cover Design by:
Ken Raney

Interior Design by:
Chris Treccani
www.3dogcreative.net

In an effort to support local communities, raise awareness and funds, Morgan James Publishing donates a percentage of all book sales for the life of each book to Habitat for Humanity Peninsula and Greater Williamsburg.

Get involved today! Visit
www.MorganJamesBuilds.com

To my beautiful bride, Lori, who with love and determination encouraged the words out of my heart and onto the pages.

TABLE OF CONTENTS

THE SPIRIT OF HOSPITALITY

Hos·pi·tal·i·ty (Häspəˈtalətē/)

What is the definition of Hospitality?
1. Generous and friendly treatment of visitors and guests; hospitable treatment.
2. The activity of providing food, drinks, etc. for people who are the guests or customers of an organization. *(Source, Merriam-Webster)*

Noun: hospitality
1. The friendly and generous reception and entertainment of guests, visitors, or strangers.
- Synonyms ~ Friendliness, hospitableness, warm reception, welcome, helpfulness, neighborliness, warmth, kindness, congeniality, geniality, cordiality, courtesy, amenability, gererosity, entertainment, catering, food "we found nothing but hospitality among the local inhabitants." *(Google Definition)*

Hospitality refers to the relationship between a guest and a host, wherein the host receives the guest with goodwill, including the reception and entertainment of guests, visitors, or strangers. Louis, chevalier de Jaucourt describes hospitality in the Encyclopedia as the virtue of a great soul that cares for the whole universe through the ties of humanity. *(Wikipedia)*

The spirit of hospitality is caught, not taught.
LARRY STUART HOSPITALITY

INTRODUCTION

Hospitality doesn't start at the restaurant or hotel or airline. It starts at home. In everyday life. Because life is all about being hospitable. Some, like E.M. Statler, would call it a life of service. The spirit of hospitality is caught, not taught. There's no such thing as turning on the hospitality. You either own it and walk in it, or you don't. The motivation behind walking in a spirit of hospitality and offering that to another person comes from the heart. One intentionally provides an act of kindness. It's the difference between the server who is only going through the motions versus the one who approaches your table with a sincere smile and provides his best service because he's passionate about his job and enjoys interacting with the guests he serves.

Somewhere along the way, this value of kindness when serving others has become a lost art. Maybe life has become so busy we don't have time to stop and serve others. Or maybe we've just lost touch with hospitality, period. A lot has changed over the past few generations, and some of those changes have brought our current hospitality conundrum with them.

I grew up in the generation known as the Baby Boomers. For most, Mom doted on us while Dad worked his hardest to provide our suburban house with its white picket fence. Our post-war economy thrived, and we lived the American Dream. We Boomers knew we were special, because Mom and Dad told us that all the time. As we grew into our late teens and twenties, we decided to take off and do what we wanted. Life was all about us, and an era of rebellion began.

By the time we started having children and Generation X arrived, serving our fellow man out of a heart of love was no longer an everyday occurrence. Instead of training our children to love one another and treat each other with kindness, we still focused on ourselves and our felt needs. Divorce rates grew, and our kids were stuck holding the short end of the straw. Since they didn't know any better, life became all about them as well. Bullying increased, divorce continued to increase, and the generation to follow, the Millennials, has been designated a generation of entitled kids who live at home until they're thirty-something. This generation has also decided everyone should get along despite their differences, and that they want their work to have meaning or they'd rather not work at all. Maybe the Millennials will be instrumental in bringing the spirit of hospitality back into the hospitality industry.[1]

Technology has also afforded changes in our shopping habits and the arena of guest service. With a credit card and the press of a button, we can have anything our heart desires. Thanks to express mail, we can have it the next day. Hungry and busy? Fast food and microwaves save time. Want the best price on a hotel, flight, or rental car? We can book them all online within seconds. The world has taken the human touch out of the guest service process, thanks to the technological revolution. As patrons of hospitality, we must pledge to never let technology diminish or replace the human touch.

To top it off, businesses attempt to cut costs by replacing guest service representatives with digital menus. Have you ever needed to ask a live person a question about your account and found yourself chasing a digital tail in circles just trying to get through to one? Press one for X. Press two for Y. And if you're lucky, Z will lead you to the person you need to talk with and there won't be a twenty-minute hold. I disagree with this approach to cutting costs. It's taking the cheap way out, and because of it, guest service has declined. Even if you do make it through to a live person, they may not be able to help you. But maybe the next person they connect you to will have the answer you need. Or maybe not. Unfortunately, robotic guest service can never come close to satisfying a guest.

So, what's lacking in the business world? The answer is simpler than one may presume. The spirit of hospitality represents the extraordinary ingredients that are necessary for a business' success in today's world. Can businesses get by without improving their guest service? Sure, and many do. But the spirit of hospitality is what will separate the good from the great.

Throughout the remainder of this book, we will discuss what it looks like to own a spirit of hospitality and how it applies to business. You'll learn what the key ingredients are and what business should taste like when these ingredients work together. We'll talk about how to build a winning team and the opportunities that will come from their excellent guest service.

A spirit of hospitality includes seven key ingredients: team unity, encouragement, accountability, kindness, generosity, humility, and gratitude. The recipe is all about character. If any one of these ingredients is missing, it leaves a guest desiring more. But when all are included in the blend, the experience is very satisfying.

The question on all of our minds is, "What about my bottom line?" We want to know whether or not business will improve if we incorporate the aforementioned ingredients of the spirit of hospitality. The short answer is, "Yes." If you read this book and implement the concepts, your bottom line will increase.

An idea is worth a buck. Making it happen is worth a million!
LARRY STUART HOSPITALITY

Building the Spirit of Hospitality

*In this ever-changing society, the most powerful and enduring brands
are built from the heart. They are real and sustainable.
Their foundations are stronger because they are built with the strength
of the human spirit, not an ad campaign.
The companies that are lasting are those that are authentic.*
- HOWARD SHULTZ

A clear definition of our corporate culture sets the stage for the entire hospitality program. What does our company stand for? Can we clearly present that to our team members? Does everyone recognize it from the CEO all the way down to the busser or the sanitation engineer? It's very important for the spirit of hospitality to be central to the company's culture so everyone who experiences the company's service—from leadership to guest—will recognize it as soon as they interact with someone from our organization.

If our team members don't know or agree with our corporate culture, they will always make mistakes or buck the system. Our values need to stand out. We need to reinforce them with our actions, our words, and our reactions. Just like our mission statement, we need to eat, sleep, and breathe our spirit of hospitality culture.

Consider Trader Joe's, Southwest Airlines, and Chick-fil-A. What's their culture? It's their pleasure to serve others. You'll rarely see a frown when you walk to the counter. Their team members smile. When a guest calls in with a question or concern, he can hear that smile through the phone. They enjoy working. They ask for a guest's name and then respond with it, making us feel very special when engaging with them. People aren't just the next check adding to their cash flow. We are individuals with individual needs, and they recognize that. The environment is relaxed, welcoming, and kindness oozes from every fiber of the team. Their entire hospitality production works because every team member understands and agrees with their corporate culture—or they wouldn't have been hired in the first place.

We need to be sure to hire team members who will serve our culture to our guests. They will either have the spirit of hospitality, or they won't. It's the responsibility of our HR team to protect the value of our culture through the vetting process. Throughout my career, I've always hired a smile first, a positive attitude second, and a willingness to do whatever it takes third. We can train skill sets, but we can't train the spirit of hospitality. Our goal is to bring our entire operation to a level of service that our guests deserve.

At Texas Roadhouse, they consider one another to be family. "We take care of each other." They promote a culture of flexible work schedules in order to balance work and home life. If someone needs to work from home, they try to accommodate that. The heart and soul of their culture is their core values of passion, partnership, integrity, and fun—and all of those have a purpose.[2] Like Texas Roadhouse has done, we need to create a culture our team members will find value in and appreciate. When we do so, turnover decreases and productivity, morale, and commitment increase.

Vision and Mission

In 1962, President Kennedy was visiting NASA headquarters for the first time. While touring the facility, he introduced himself to a janitor who was mopping the floor and asked him what he was doing. He replied, "Well, Mr. President, I'm helping put a man on the moon."

Good companies possess a strong sense of what they're all about and communicate that purpose to each and every team member. People in today's workforce need to know they're contributing to something meaningful. Within the next twenty years, the millennial generation will comprise the majority of the workforce. Millennials want to know that they are serving a greater purpose in whatever they put their hands to do. Without a strong mission statement, our team won't know why they're working from nine to five every day. That will lead to turnover, because they won't stay in a position they're not passionate about. Give them a sense of meaning by pointing them toward your mission statement.

If our people don't feel as if they're part of the recipe of our company or know the direction they're supposed to go—the mission of the company—they will never become committed to working as if they are stakeholders and will find themselves going in circles. Eventually, they will quit. Our company's mission statement is the compass team members will turn to for direction. What's the company's center? That's the direction people usually miss. We understand North, South, East, and West. But what's at the center of those directions? If our team members know what the center focus is, they can make wise decisions concerning varying aspects of their jobs based on that center focus. And that's when we find corporate success. Everyone in our company should have one collective mission that puts us working toward one goal. Whether the team member is part of the maintenance staff, food and beverage, or housekeeping or they are part of the IT staff, marketing, or the executive team, he or she should know they are an important part of achieving the mission statement's goal through their individual efforts.

Have you ever seen video footage of Southwest's flight attendants "performing" their pre-flight instructions to the passengers? Do you have room in your seat on a full Southwest flight? Are their boarding times shorter and sweeter than those of other airlines? If you answered yes to all or even most of these questions, then you know they're living up to their mission statement. Their team members are effectively working as a team and creating a fun environment for their guests to enjoy.

The key to the success of your company, whether it be the accomplishments of your team members, successfully satisfying guests, or the success of your overall return on investment is dependent on your mission statement and everyone's ability to achieve that mission. There are several ways to get that mission statement in front of your team:

- Talk about it every chance you get. It needs to be communicated multiple times on a daily basis. Bring it up during morning meetings, conferences, and staff reviews.
- Include it in your email signature.
- Post it in the staff break room.
- Find creative ways to comment about it in general conversations with team members.

Everyone who works for our company needs to eat, sleep, and breathe it. When it's internalized, our team members will serve our guests successfully out of a natural desire to fulfill our corporate mission, thus improving our bottom line.

Finding Success in the Hospitality Industry

We have all been blessed with talents and a purpose in life. In the hospitality industry, our passions include but are not limited to serving others, smiling, welcoming others into our establishments and homes, helping others by exceeding a need, entertaining, encouraging, making others feel good despite their circumstances, and offering a little more. If we aren't passionate about a life of service, then we're in the wrong industry and need to consider a career change. If we want to pursue a career in the hospitality industry, then we need to ignite a passion within our careers. Once that passion is in play, there are three keys to achieving success:

- Success always starts with a plan.
- Success requires commitment.
- Surround yourself with people who share your values.

Success Always Starts with a Plan

Success always starts with designing a plan and then following through with it. A blueprint to build a career from the ground up. When we are building hotel or restaurant brands, we need to know every detail from the critical path time frame, feasibility study, budget, business plan, and labor requirements to the design criteria, Furniture Fixtures & Equipment, materials, menu, and so much more. And in order to know these things, we need to have an intimate knowledge of today's business demand that we're passionate about.

I spent many years helping to design and build restaurants. In the 1990s, I was hired to participate in the design development of the twelve Walt Disney World Dolphin restaurants and lounges, working alongside Tishman Construction, who built Walt Disney World, the World Trade Center, and many other behemoth projects. One cannot find success in such massive projects without having and executing a solid business plan. And to create that viable plan, you have to know your business inside and out.

Prior to the Walt Disney World Dolphin, I led operations building teams in over twelve restaurants. My friend, partner, and hotel mentor, Octavio Gomez, remembered how I had served him in the entertainment business in the 1970s. Octavio was Regional Director of Food and Beverage on the East Coast for Sheraton Corporation. When he was offered the opportunity to become the resident manager of the Walt Disney World Dolphin, because of our previous business relationship, he knew I was the perfect fit to provide an entertainment/hospitality leadership flair. As Director of Restaurants, I provided the necessary development support with the themes, the story lines, the service style for each restaurant, culinary direction and menu planning.

What did the plan require? First, a committed willingness to take the position. This was the career move that paved the way for my future success. Second, it took pure creativity. I saw what each space could be because of the opportunities previous jobs I'd held had presented. The story for each restaurant had to come first. Then, we hired and trained the staff. The guest experience had to be above and beyond the rest—better known as Disneyesque. My entertainment background combined with my schooling at Cornell and subsequent hotel/restaurant experience gave me the credentials and ability to execute at the highest level of performance.

Success Requires Commitment

Coming up with and executing a plan doesn't only require vision and knowledge. It also requires the total giving of one's self in all that we commit to. We have to give to get, and we have to work to eat. We must be fully involved and fully invested. If we aren't, an area of our foundation is going to be weak, which could tumble the entire operation. When we aren't fully involved, it leaves room for mistakes, and in this business of building a kingdom, mistakes are costly.

Servant leaders have skill sets that are foundational to their position: planning, organization, and administration. They must be prepared to execute a plan at any time. Once we're invested and our plan is developed, it must be followed. We need to be sure our goals are scheduled daily and achievable. They should lead us one step at a time toward success.

Once I was hired to design and operate the Walt Disney World Dolphin restaurants, I got to work. It would take six months of planning before the hotel even opened. For me, having the honor of being part of the Walt Disney World Dolphin team meant having a to-do-list for every single day. I worked on a team with respected leaders, and we worked together to get the one-of-a-kind concept off the ground. We procured all the necessary equipment, hired the best service professionals and culinary talent, married unique flavors to complement each of our outlets, and created a memorable dining experience with a Disneyesque entertainment flair for our guests.

Surround Yourself with People Who Share Your Values

When things came together at the Walt Disney World Dolphin, the executive team worked closely with me and others to make any necessary changes. Regardless of whether we're working toward our own goals or helping someone else achieve theirs, we are surrounded by people.

Building a restaurant (or reinventing one) requires our personal vision and creativity to get the plan outlined and signed off on, but it takes a team of others to achieve it. In other words, we're surrounded by people who are part of our success or failure. The key is to surround yourself with people who share your value system.

There are always going to be people who don't see eye to eye with us or we don't see eye to eye with them, but if we are surrounded by people who think the way we do, we have far more chance of success than if we surround ourselves with people who are always going to challenge our authority or rebel against our ideas. That doesn't mean we don't listen to ideas presented as constructive criticism. We need those people to challenge us to rise higher and overcome our own weaknesses. But we should avoid the people who suck the life out of us or are always contrary. They aren't going to encourage our success and may likely be jealous when it comes. Remember, surround yourself with people who share your values.

When we build our business on these foundational principles, threading the spirit of hospitality throughout, we have a wonderful chance at finding success and a return on our investment. The spirit of hospitality is not intended to be a reaction to guest needs, but instead a sincere, proactive effort toward building positive relationships by serving our guests from the heart. It is the key to success in any business, whether that business is a hotel, an airline, a restaurant, or the grocery store. No matter where your office is located, if you want to have a successful business, you must master the spirit of hospitality *first*—and so must your team.

TAKEOUT:

▸ In order for our company to find success, we must be fully committed to the mission statement. So must our team members.

▸ When we live the spirit of hospitality, our ideas become reality.

▸ All it takes is a plan, commitment, and the right people to build our business and increase our bottom line.

Your word and character are all you're worth,
so how do you value your name?
LARRY STUART HOSPITALITY

Integrity and the Spirit of Hospitality

Leadership is doing what is right when no one is watching.
— GEORGE VAN VALKENBURG

By definition, integrity is the quality of being honest and having strong moral principles. It's having a moral uprightness. Integrity is standing up for what is right. It's doing the right things for the right reasons that bring the right results. There are two roads one can take in business: the narrow road of serving others with excellence or the wide road of doing your own thing. Without integrity, there's no moral foundation upon which to build a life of value. We cannot be an example of the spirit of hospitality if we don't possess a strong character, consistently operating in the qualities of humility, honesty, and sincerity, doing so with a servant's heart.

People who walk in the spirit of hospitality put others before themselves. They treat others with kindness. They say they're going to do something and then they do it. They keep their word and their promises. Their yes is yes and their no is no. They are consistent, faithful, loyal, unbending in their moral convictions. These people are the types of people we all want to work for or have working for us. They're people we can trust, knowing they will always do the right thing and will never intentionally let us down. Their motives are pure, because they have heart and are entrepreneurial go-getters.

Chick-fil-A is closed on Sunday because its founder, S. Truett Cathy, believed in putting others before himself. He operated his businesses under biblical principles, which included taking a day to allow his team members to rest and enjoy their families. He believed in raising up a next generation of servant leaders, evidenced in his WinShape programs. He was a humble man who understood the meaning of a life of integrity. Not only was he dedicated to building a successful business, he was dedicated to his family.[3] When we read articles about Chick-fil-A and their success, we find honorable information. Their humble service produces such a profit that they are currently listed as the top limited-service restaurant by the ACSI—two years in a row.[4]

The restaurant at the bottom of that list focused on franchising more than the quality of its food and the speed of its service. Thus, the brand suffers inconsistency. No two restaurants provide equal service, and one never knows how long they may be sitting in the drive-through line waiting for service or their food. Plus, chances are the guest won't receive exactly what he ordered.

I ask again, which of these has made the spirit of hospitality an integral part of their business? When we fail to walk in integrity, to walk the talk, our guests lose trust in us and will find someplace else to put it. Operating with honor and integrity while upholding the highest quality business standards will separate the excellent from the mediocre.

A Good Name

Think about people you know, whether they are family, friends, co-workers, celebrities, or executives in leadership. What stands out about them? More importantly, when you think of their name, do you associate it with integrity? Good character? In business, company name matters, and so does the man or woman standing behind that company name and the men and women standing behind them, upholding that brand. The question we have to ask ourselves is, am I a man or woman of integrity?

A life without integrity can leave us tossed back and forth without any direction. Greed overtakes the desire to maintain a good name. With integrity, we're anchored with honor and character, strong morals, positive family values, a powerful work ethic, and humility.

Our word is of great worth in the business world and in life. Consider how many times someone has said they would help with something and then backed out at last minute or simply forgot to get it done. How did that leave you feeling? Disappointed? Frustrated? Maybe their lack of follow-through cost you or your business something. Keeping our word and being able to have someone count on us is critical for our integrity. It's easy to build a good name by following through on what we say we'll do.

Doing the Right Thing for the Right Reason

Integrity is also about always doing the right thing for the right reason. In the hospitality industry, we deal with a vast variety of people every day. There is no manual containing all of the right answers for every situation. Every now and then we will need to decide whether to go above and beyond company policies in order to exceed a guest's expectations, and that isn't always going to be an easy decision. But if we walk in integrity, we will always do the right thing in order to bless our guest with our superior guest service delivery. Will it possibly cost us or the company? Yes. Is it worth it? Always.

In May of 2015, a passenger was on a flight when the airline received a call from her husband to let her know their son had slipped into a coma after an accident. Southwest turned the plane around, took her back to the terminal, rebooked her without additional fees, and had her on the next non-stop flight out to Denver, where her son was hospitalized. The airline could have had several disgruntled passengers whose flight was delayed, but they counted a mother's cost as more important than their own.[5] This is doing the right thing for the right reason.

Excellence

A standard is a degree or level of requirement, excellence, or attainment. What is your standard of excellence? Do you set the bar high enough for your team to strive for excellence but low enough to allow room for mistakes and the grace to follow with gentle correction, redirection, or more training? We should always lead others in a spirit of excellence. It's important for that standard to be set so that our service comes across as natural, yet professional. We must strive to be the best at whatever we seek to accomplish.

Our spirit of excellent service makes things happen in peoples' lives to improve their day or their way of living, whether we're interacting with a guest or a fellow team member. The difference between ordinary and extraordinary is a little extra. In the hospitality industry, that little extra will always produce an improved return on investment.

Commitment

Commitment is lacking in our world today. It starts in the lower grades when a child joins a sports team and quits halfway through the season because he or she isn't winning or decides it's not for her. Rather than making the child stick it out and learn the value of commitment or seeing something through to the end, the parents let the child walk away. "They're young. Let them try something else," is the common reasoning. Eventually, the parent hopes, something will stick.

In college, we see it in the form of changing majors. In a career, we see it in the form of job hopping. Don't like your spouse anymore? Get a divorce. The minute we find something we don't like, we drop it like a hot potato and move on to the next best thing. To be winners, all we need to give is all we have. We must be able to stand by our commitments and see them through.

Integrity will always go further than output. If the foundation is integral and sincere and genuine, it lasts and will be remembered forever. Output lasts for a day. Guests come and guests go. We come to work. We serve. We go home. Our output—what we do—only lasts for that moment. But if we treat others with kindness, genuine care, and a heart of service, they will remember that and will return. Because that foundation lasts a lifetime. If we make a mistake, but our intention was sincere, a guest or co-worker or leader will recognize that sincerity, in which case grace is easily offered. They will know that our heart was in the right place. And that matters far more than any mishap. But if that intention was in any way selfish or greedy, it's likely we'll lose that guest and our service will ultimately fail. Without integrity as the foundation, businesses will crumble. It won't take long for our guests to realize that we're all about making money and could care less about them and their concerns. Guests who feel unimportant may share their story with the rest of the world, negatively impacting our brand, which in turn makes us the biggest loser.

TAKEOUT:

In order for our business to succeed, we must:

- ▸ Build it on a granite foundation of integrity.
- ▸ Remain committed to our company culture and our individual positions within it.
- ▸ Serve with a spirit of hospitality excellence.
- ▸ Always choose to do the right thing for the right reason, no matter the cost.

*The spirit of hospitality doesn't turn on at work.
It's a habit, a lifestyle. It's always on.
It's always about serving others first.*
LARRY STUART HOSPITALITY

3

Hiring the Spirit of Hospitality

Ability is what you're capable of doing.
Motivation determines what you do.
Attitude determines how you do it.
– LOU HOLTZ

As we stated in chapter two, the most valuable possession anyone or any business has is its name. Depending on the character of either, our name will be known among others as good or not-so-great or outright horrible. Before we consider hiring a potential team member, we need to evaluate which name we want for our business. Consider those entities whose guest service stands out in your mind. What makes them the best at what they do? The bottom line is that it's their quality guest service. It's what you experienced when you made a purchase, stayed at their hotel, flew from New York City to Los Angeles, or dined at their restaurant. When hiring team members, the key is to find the right people who are dynamically passionate about having a good name. And that starts with your business.

Passion for Your Business

If you've been in business in the past twenty-plus years, you've likely heard the term "business culture" or "organizational culture." According to businessdictionary.com, this is defined as "the values and behaviors that contribute to the unique social and psychological environment of an organization."[6] Knowing that, consider Walt Disney World. What's their culture? Family friendly. Hospitable. Ethnic diversity. Fun for all ages. When you pay big bucks to take your family of four to a Walt Disney property, you know you're going to have a full experience. Themed hotels, diverse foods from various countries, the rides and thrills of the theme park, and fireworks to end the day. Their staff will be friendly, engaging, and they'll smile when your eyes meet. You'll see characters you've loved and known for decades and generations. Disney has created a culture that spans generations. When they hire cast members, they look for qualities in those people that exemplify their standards and expectations. If a person were to walk into an interview for a position in the Walt Disney kingdom with a sour face, they'll likely not be considered a good fit. Their exterior impression doesn't fit the Disney culture.

When hiring team members, be sure they're passionate about life, their purpose, and their career goals. If they aren't, they're not likely to uphold your business' culture. The staff is the most critical component of your business, because the team members mirror the representation and image of your organization's spirit and brand. Whatever defines your particular company needs to be found within the people you hire to bring that reality to fruition. And their passion needs to come from their heart, not their head. Heart passion lasts a lifetime. If the team member only loves the idea of the job, their passion won't last.

It's important to recognize that a life of service is about looking outward rather than inward, understanding that life isn't about me. It's about other people. Too often we hire entitled team members who are there to build their ego and make their paycheck but have no other investment in the company or their crew members in the workplace. Service isn't a word in their vocabulary. They see themselves as being above serving others. They're entitled to their paycheck, but they do the minimum required to get the job done and get paid. Unfortunately, this is a result of being handed everything in life without having to work for it or to compete for it. Sure, we're all special, but that doesn't mean we stop striving to better ourselves and serve our fellow man. Selfishness is not a quality we want in our profession.

For one job, we hired a great PR guy instead of the food and beverage executive my leadership team intended to hire. We assumed he had all the necessary experience and skill sets—planning, administration, and organization. He snuck in through HR, who had identified him as the best in show for a particular hospitality leadership role. Time went by, and we received feedback from our team that we had an ill-equipped leader who lacked the spirit of hospitality. He was all about himself and neglected providing the necessary support to lead and guide the team in a way that would provide the memorable guest experience to the end user, our guests. At that point, the damage had already been done.

When hiring, the pattern tends toward "be quick, but don't hurry."[7] We have a position to fill but don't always have the right candidate available. What ends up happening is that we get a guy through an interview who knew how to sell himself but isn't made of the spirit of hospitality DNA of our team. The issue then becomes our personal or corporate credibility. It ends up on the line because that guy works under us. When the wrong people come through our door, we have to nip their positions in the bud ASAP so minimal damage is done. As leaders and human resources department team members, we must beware the wolf in sheep's clothing. They look like a perfect fit on the outside, but they lack the character necessary to uphold the spirit of hospitality inside. They want to be part of the glory of the project, but the credit is never passed on to others because it's all about them. The vetting process needs to be stringent to ensure the spirit of hospitality, the foundation of our core value system, is protected. It's never wrong to do our research and conduct thorough background checks of everyone we look at potentially filling a position in our company. Selfishness is a damaging ingredient that's running rampant in our industry. Hiring someone who is all about themselves and not a team player—who considers themselves to be all that and a bag of chips— is like not paying attention and putting cups of salt and teaspoons of sugar into the cookie batter.

In order to serve others, we have to be willing to deny ourselves. That's the greatest form of compassion, and our guests will want to know we genuinely care about them if we want them to return to our establishment. In order to build a successful team, we must hire quality individuals who understand the difference between doing their job and serving other people from our hearts. The first will only do what is required to keep their job. The latter will strive to serve with excellence as a productive member of the hospitality team. It's easy to find good-looking individuals who have it all on the outside but have no idea how to put aside selfish ambition and strive for a higher purpose. Others may have a resume filled with experience, but if they don't have an ounce of humility, they won't be a strong team player.

Passion for the Job

The spirit of hospitality doesn't turn on at work. It's a habit, a lifestyle. It's always on. It's always about serving others first. Consider your passions in life. I'm willing to bet most of them revolve around the service industry. Does being around other people energize you? Do you love to see the reaction when you make someone's day special? Are you the type of person most others despise because you carry joy in your heart and you can't help but smile? Life is good, and your cup's half full—or better yet, it's overflowing. This is the type of person who would find fulfillment in a career in the hospitality industry. This is the person who resembles the movie character Annie, the complete opposite of her rival, Miss Hannigan. This person's sun will always come out tomorrow, and the hard-knock life is what they make of it. Lemons will quickly become lemonade when this person is serving you, your business, and your clientele. This person has passion for and is committed to life. They cherish and serve our guests with the spirit of hospitality.

A life of service executed with the spirit of hospitality is the difference one experiences when we truly enjoy what we do. We need to be sure our potential hires are pursuing a career they will enjoy. One they are passionate about. We don't want him to be the guy who is so unhappy behind the front desk that he's always checking his watch. Or the woman who's so unhappy making beds that she's taking twice as long to clean the room and therefore unproductive. We need to ask our potential team members what they are passionate about and encourage them to pursue that, even if it isn't a position in the hospitality industry. If they are serving in the arena they were called to from birth, they'll enjoy their work and find success.

A Solid Work Ethic

We've heard a lot in our lifetime about how people don't want to work. They're entitled and they want everything handed to them on a silver platter. They're also lazy and only do as much as needed to get by. Forget going the extra mile—they don't understand that concept anymore. Whatever happened to work ethic? It may not be as extinct as we think.

As we discovered in the beginning of this book, our culture has taken a turn from generation to generation. Traditionalists, who understood the meaning of personal responsibility and pulling one for the team, are leaving this world and taking much of that work ethic with them. Baby Boomers are living out their retirement or taking on second careers as they find themselves in need of income in order to make due. Or they're choosing not to retire. Generation Xers are either thriving in their career or still searching for one. Millennials are flooding the workforce after either earning a degree or deciding it's time to get off of Mom and Dad's couch and do something with their lives.[8] While each generation has its slackers, not all is lost. Fortunately, Millennials want their work to have purpose. They want to know they're making a difference in the world rather than just going to a job. If we can find those who have a passion for the hospitality industry, we've hit a goldmine.

What constitutes a good work ethic?

- ▸ Being on time.
- ▸ Dressing appropriately.
- ▸ Doing more than what's required.

- Getting along with others despite differences.
- Commitment.
- Being willing to learn.
- Recognizing you don't know it all.
- Admitting mistakes.
- Taking ownership of responsibility.
- Being self-motivated and not standing around waiting for direction during a lull in service.

People who understand work ethics will do the menial tasks because they need to be done. It's a rarity these days to find someone who will stop for thirty seconds and pick up the paper towels from the bathroom floor before they wash their hands to return to work. They're working to live rather than living to work, and they are still out there. It's our job as team leaders to find them. It's always better to fill the position with someone who has a passion for their job than someone who's just there to make a paycheck and go home.

A People Person

The most contagious spirit is enthusiasm.
– LARRY STUART HOSPITALITY

To serve is to be engaged in the people business. Think back to our Annie reference earlier. Granted, not everyone has a sunny personality, but a sunny disposition is a must for the servant in the hospitality industry. Team members must be "people persons." In the hospitality industry, we are always interacting, whether it's with co-workers, guests, or vendors. If we cannot do our job with a spirit of hospitality, executing genuine guest service, we will fail our team and our guests. Someone who is personable will work with a whatever-it-takes, lay-down-my-life-for-others attitude. These are the people who willingly go the extra mile without thinking twice about what it will cost them.

Enthusiasm provides the edge over the competition when applying for work, building friendships, or being the go-to person for those in need. People gravitate toward those who are excited and have a positive outlook on life, whose glass is always half full, despite the circumstances surrounding them. Enthusiastic people make others feel good about themselves and bring an energy that vitalizes those around them. It's contagious. Enthusiastic people will bring the ever-important positive attitude that will affect change in the atmosphere when the work day seems it won't ever end.

The Most Beautiful Attire is a Smile

A smile is your calling card. I've always said that you can buy someone's back and hands, but you can't buy their smile. Many will be willing to do the physical work, but they may not be passionate enough that it transfers to their presentation and execution. It's easy to hire individuals who have it all on the outside but don't have a clue how to serve their fellow man.

When hiring the spirit of hospitality, a natural, welcoming smile is a priority. Without it, your guest won't feel welcomed, cared for, or appreciated. One man I know has his human resources personnel judge a potential team member's smile on a scale of one to ten. If their smile doesn't score an eight or higher, they're automatically cut. A smile cannot be trained. It comes from the heart. If someone can't smile, they need to look for a job someplace else—outside of the hospitality industry.

A smile can create a positive moment in the midst of tears, unhappiness, or stress. It brings a person's personality to life. It adds a special sparkle. It's a universal connection here on earth. A smile will, most of the time, attract another smile. Smiles are gifts that don't cost anything to give and are valuable to receive. Especially for the person who is having a challenging day. Smiles are a sign of encouragement and love. A smile is key requirement when hiring someone who will be serving others.

Humility

Serving others doesn't always come naturally, nor does a servant's heart develop overnight. It cannot easily be trained later in life. Just as the cliché says, it's difficult to teach old dogs new tricks. It's even more difficult to teach a person how to serve with the spirit of hospitality if they haven't grown up in an environment where that was taught and nurtured from a young age. But it is possible for someone to develop the heart of a servant if they have a willingness to learn to put others first. Note that it takes a very special, compassionate, patient person to accept this not-so-easy task.

Finding someone who possesses humility is all about identifying individuals who are sincere, love themselves enough to love others, are willing to do whatever it takes to serve each other, and most importantly, will hold themselves accountable to use their God-given talents to the best of their ability. Skill sets, education, and goals can be learned through various training processes. But team members cannot always learn to have a spirit of hospitality. It's always best to hire someone who naturally walks in it already.

Finding the Perfect Team

Eighty percent of your possible perfect-fit team members are going to come through the front door via Human Resources. I would encourage your hiring team to identify people who embody the qualities we've discussed thus far and then train those people to do the tasks required of them. We can always train the tasks, but we can't always train the spirit of hospitality. It's caught. Not taught.

It's also important that our new hires are going to work well with those who are already winning at serving as part of our team. Some of our companies have three of their team members panel interview the potential new hire to find out if he or she will work well with the already-existing team.

Knowing which position we're hiring the new team member to fill is also important because positioning is key. We don't want a non-people person in the front of the house where they need to be on-stage ready.

They'd better serve in the back, where the only people they'll need to interact with are co-workers. If we find that someone we're hiring to serve as wait staff has a passion for the culinary side of our business, maybe we need to consider hiring them to work the back of the house or kitchen instead. It's not unheard of to create a position for the right person, rather than trying too hard to find the right person for the position.

So, where do we find these people who don't come through the front door?

Major job fairs are a great place to find new staff. During a mass-hiring initiative, we have the opportunity to interview thousands of people and select the few hundred who possess the spirit of hospitality. How do we do that with only a day or two to interview all those people? There are seven key ingredients I looked for when hiring in a mass-market arena.

2. **Do they look the part?** First impressions matter when considering so many candidates at one time. The potential team member must be dressed in a professional manner—no holes in the jeans, no revealing tops, etc. Have you ever had someone walk past you or up to you smelling like sweat? Not pleasant. Is the person well groomed? These aren't the only physical characteristics I look for when speed hiring, though.

3. **Is their smile natural?** If it is, it shows in their eyes. It's part of who they are, not something they put on in order to attempt to get a job. It should be their calling card. Knowing if their smile is sincere or not is the key.

4. **Are they personable?** It's easy to read a person's body language. Personable people will lean toward whoever they're talking to, rather than away from them. Crossed arms are usually a sign of stubbornness or protection of self, although if it's chilly, the person may simply be cold. Are they making positive and engaging eye contact? Or are they distracted by everything happening around them? These are all ways to tell if a person is going to be a wonderful servant or not.

5. **What's reflected in their tone?** The way someone says something is going to be incredibly important when they are communicating with a guest. Especially if our business involves a lot of phone conversations. We want to work with people who are enthusiastic, gentle, and polite when speaking, not harsh and rude. Are they articulating or are they bumbling over their answers? We may be able to teach them the proper thing to say, but we won't be able to train their tone.

6. **Are they passionate about the service industry?** This will be evident in their conversation, and a seasoned professional will easily identify it.

7. **Do they possess the skills necessary to do their job?** These are trainable skills, so it isn't a deal breaker if the interviewee needs to learn a few new skills. Better to fill the position with someone who has the spirit of hospitality and a passion for other people but may need to learn the skills than it is to fill the position with someone who knows how to do it all but is irritable in spirit.

8. **Is their attitude positive?** Are they willing to do whatever it takes to accomplish excellent guest service? This is critical, as this sets apart the people who are willing to learn, adopt the business culture, and treat co-workers and guests with respect and honor.

9. **What is their character like?** You may not be able to identify this up front. They may have to prove it over a period of time. When you speak with the people your potential team member has listed as references, make certain to ask if they walk in integrity, honor others, uphold their responsibilities, and readily admit their mistakes.

Not every company has the luxury of hiring via a job fair or convention. If you don't, then you need to find quality team members where you are. The same key ingredients should be observed in anyone you will meet locally. When you find a person with the spirit of hospitality at the local grocery store, on vacation, at the coffee shop, at your place of worship, or at the local college, have a conversation with them. Ask how long they've worked where they're currently employed. Find out their short- and long-term goals. Ask if they've ever considered working in the hospitality industry. Let them know you've identified a spirit of hospitality in them and that it would be your pleasure to further discuss some opportunities you have within your company. Pass them a business card, and if they're open to it, request their contact information. Give them a couple of days to consider your offer, and if you haven't heard from them, give them a call. Remind them of your offer and ask if they have any questions or concerns. What's the worst they can say? "No thank you."

If the prospective team member is interested, guide them into your internship program. Once they work with others who fully operate in the spirit of hospitality, they won't ever want to leave because they'll end up loving what they do. This builds confidence and morale amongst your team, and growth becomes evident in productivity and performance.

Finally, before allowing a new team member to take any position, ask discerning questions to be sure the job is going to be the perfect fit for their skill set, attitude, and character. Make sure not only your expectations are going to be met, but that theirs are as well. Or make sure you or they are willing to adjust expectations accordingly in order to obtain a win-win result.

Proper Positioning

Once we've identified the individuals who will best fit our team, it's time to identify the right position for them to fill. This may seem the reverse of most hiring processes. Typically, we have a position we need to fill, and we search for someone to fill it. A better goal would be to find the right person for our team and provide them with a position. This will reduce turnover, saving the company money in the long run, as well as providing an opportunity for profit.

Your team members' dreams are more a part of the process than you realize. When considering them for a position, ask them about themselves. What does your potential team member love to do? What are their hobbies?

Certain skills are needed for different hobbies. If they love to play chess, they will be thinking ahead and calculating their next move. If they love to craft, they will be creative, able to see things before they come to life. If they enjoy sports, they may have a competitive side, which may push them to get ahead of the crowd. Knowing the answer to these questions will direct you toward their gifts and talents and provide you with an understanding of their potential purpose as members of your team.

Some people may not recognize their own gifts and talents. Maybe we employers may not know ours as well—at least not beyond the surface level. How does one discover their gifts? It's easier than we may think.

1. **Consider childhood.** What did you love to do as a kid? What interested you to the degree that you consistently pursued it? For me, it was passing time serving others or serving alongside other servants at the hotels my father frequented during his entertainment career. I had no problem helping to clear tables, pick up towels at the pool, make beds, or park cars as I grew through my teen years. I truly enjoyed the world of hospitality and being part of a productive team.

2. **What makes time fly for you?** What do you find yourself immersed in to the degree that you lose track of time? Is it spending time in the kitchen? Watching cooking shows? Trying new recipes? Pinning recipes and cooking tips? Notice the pattern here? This person would probably make a great chef.

3. **What are you passionate about?** What could you spend all day talking about? Or doing? Or studying? This is an ingrained part of who you are—it's in your DNA. That is a good starting point for what you'd love to do as a career, because you'll never tire of it.

4. **What do others say you're good at?** Sometimes we have to get past ourselves to discover who we truly are and what we're capable of. Our excuses can get in the way of our dreams far too often. When trying to figure out what we're good at, it's important to ask those closest to us, "What do you see as my gifts or talents?" One of

my childhood neighbors and surrogate parents, Fran, saw the spirit of hospitality and my potential to work in this industry. Every year, we had Christmas dinner at her house. She remembers that I always had the napkin draped over my arm and would go around serving everyone wine. I then served the meal. If I came into the kitchen to warm up the plates, she'd move out of the way with a smile, because she knew I was passionate about food and drink and all it entailed. But more importantly, I was all about serving others. When interviewing potential service specialists, be sure to watch listen closely to their answers and go from there. You will know every time if that individual is a good fit for your business.

Finally, what is their personal goal? Not only at your company but for their life as well. Their answer will reveal a lot about their character. Are they family oriented? Do they need a balanced work/home life? Are they organized? Answers to questions like these will alert you to anything that will hinder them from productivity on the job.

When 17-year-old Ezra was let go from his job at a pizzeria for not moving fast enough at work, his parents had him take a personality test. What they discovered was that he isn't best suited for assembly line work—even in a restaurant. Having him sheet out the dough was the same tedious task over and over again. He needs work that changes up every once in a while, at least. Rather than sticking a certain personality in a position where they won't best serve and ending up with costly turnover, servant leaders should come alongside their team members and encourage them to not only be productive but also to teach them why their position is so important to the big-picture production and not just a tedious task. If we, as leaders, then discover that the individual may better serve in a different position, it would cost us less to move them into that position than it would to let them go and have to hire two new team members.

When considering a person who walks in the spirit of hospitality for a particular position, make sure it's a job their personality will enjoy doing. If not, see if there's another position you could create or fill that they would work in best. Personality tests can be helpful in finding a position that best suits a person. Check out www.16personalities.com for a quick test that will reveal a lot about your potential team member. Consider having them take it as part of the interview process. You'll be amazed at what the test will reveal about them as a worker. Then, be sure to position them properly so they will serve with a spirit of hospitality and at their top performance rate.

TAKEOUT:

It is better to hire someone who lives the spirit of hospitality and train them to do a particular job than to hire someone with the skills necessary to do the job but lacking the spirit of hospitality.

You can't train character or attitude.
LARRY STUART HOSPITALITY

4

Training the Spirit of Hospitality

We must motivate ourselves to do our very best,
and by our example lead others to do their best as well.
- TRUETT CATHY

Whether in hospitality or any other service-related business (mechanic, hairdresser, construction, etc.) where crew members are interacting with guests, from a Human Resources standpoint, it's imperative that leadership first identify individuals who possess the spirit of hospitality. Then, train them until they own the necessary skill sets to perform their job thoroughly and professionally, with the end goal of raising up servant leaders who can do the work with little or no direct supervision. It's not an easy task, for sure. But, as we say at Larry Stuart Hospitality, "An idea is worth a buck. Making it happen is worth a million."

As leaders, it's important that we set the culture at the company so that everything we do resembles putting others before ourselves. This flows from genuinely caring about those we come in contact with, and it must be at the core of what we do. There will always be issues at work, just as there are always issues in life. How we handle these issues will vary greatly based on whether or not serving others first—even our most challenging associates—is at the core of who we are and what we do. For job commitment with a purpose, we must teach character, not success, focusing on building character, not characteristics.

What does this look like in reality? While one business culture focuses on character—humility, servanthood, and kindness—another focuses on the process and convenience of the franchise. One is based on the heart of the business while the other is based on the mechanics of the business.

What can we learn from this? It starts with the leadership and flows up through the team to our guests. We can't expect our team members to follow our lead to live out the spirit of hospitality in our service to others if we don't walk the talk ourselves. We must model it by living it. We must be the first to do what we expect others to do when they're looking to us for direction and leadership. And this starts with the CEO and his leadership team, not just at the local establishment leadership level. If we want our team members to go above and beyond our expectations, we must set them up for success by leading by example and training them to do their jobs in like manner.

The more we expect from our team, the more we must cultivate their skills and focus their career objectives. Then we must empower them to do so by giving them room to make wise decisions based on what we've shown them. If we provide room for our team members to grow as entrepreneurs, they will take our company to the next level with very little direction from corporate. This can only become a reality if we allow room for trust, trials, and time. I have seen this concept accomplished multiple times over many brands I've had the honor of serving.

The way to introduce quality service standards is through a robust training program. We need to train our new team members not only in the skills necessary to do their jobs, but also in our company's culture. People need direction, as we mentioned before. Let's take a look at how to bring the best training and, therefore, the best opportunity for our team members to commit fully to their learning experiences and their subsequent jobs. We'll start with what we at Larry Stuart Hospitality call PERFORM: Purpose, Empathy, Roles and Goals, Flexibility, Optimum Show, and Recognition.

Purpose

Without vision, people don't know what they're supposed to aim for. What's our common goal? What do we want to achieve in business? What's our business philosophy? Our team members should be well aware of these, and this information should not only be central to all training, but it should also be repeated frequently throughout every day, at every staff meeting, in every email communication, and ... well, you get the point. The Ritz Carlton is known for this. At the start of their day, the Ritz Carlton teams gather for their Daily Lineup. During this fifteen-minute gathering, they do three things. They hear what is happening at a corporate level and what is happening at the local hotel—such as a memorable story of how putting their vision to work has affected a guest. They also review their twenty core values. These values are always within the team members' sight and hearing. There is never an excuse for the team members to not know how to respond in any given situation in order to accomplish the Ritz Carlton Golden Standard of Service. They are ladies and gentlemen serving ladies and gentlemen.[9]

When we're looking to hire, our potential team members need to be willing to sign off on our mission statement, agreeing that they are well aware of the standards our company strives for and are willing to exemplify those standards no matter what they are putting their hands to do any time they're on our property. The outcome of training and development of front-line crew members should reflect the values of the owners.

But knowing our business isn't enough. Team members also need to know and understand their purpose in their position. The goal is to provide a seamless delivery of our product or service. In order for that to happen, each team member needs to know what they're responsible for and how to best serve in that position. This can only happen if we point out that purpose during their training. We'll discuss this more in the upcoming section about roles and goals.

Empathy

Whether we're training our team members or they are serving guests, empathy is extremely important. People don't care how much you know until they know how much you care. It's an old adage, but it rings true in both circumstances. We must first show we care about the person we're communicating with. If we're human, we understand that when we're dealing with a difficult situation, we want someone to understand how we feel in that moment, and we don't want to be judged for feeling that way. It's a very vulnerable place to be. The knowledge that we care about their concerns also builds trust.

Unbeknownst to the hotel staff, a gentleman would be scouting their facilities for an outstanding brand in a particular industry that held annual conventions and wanted a new place to hold one. Upon his arrival, the front desk associate realized his room wasn't available due to overbooking. The gentleman hit the ceiling. When the front office leader heard the commotion, he took the initiative to come out from behind the counter, introduce himself to the guest, and profusely apologize for the oversite. He asked the gentleman if he could have a couple of minutes to resolve the issue and turn around the negative situation. Within moments, the leader had a hotel limo take the guest across the street to another of the corporation's properties, where they paid for him to spend the night. The next morning, the leader brought him back to an upgraded suite, chocolate-covered strawberries, champagne, and a written apology to him. The hotel also picked up the bill. Due to their excellent service recovery, the gentleman brought back multi-million dollar accounts. Again, the hotel staff didn't know he was scouting their property until after the fact. Yet, they took care of him as a person first.

We must train our team to consider the person first and the business second. Ask if there's something we can do to help make the person feel better. "How may I serve you?" is the appropriate hospitality statement in this situation. If the guest responds in anger, frustration, or grief—we've all seen one blow up, growl, or break down and cry at one point or another—stating that we understand their (insert emotion here) and would love to help resolve the situation will go much further than responding in like kind. This is why putting others before ourselves at all times is so incredibly important in the spirit of hospitality. It doesn't matter how ridiculous their request may sound to us. It doesn't matter whether company policy allows such-and-such response. What matters is making the guest feel important enough for someone to empathize with their felt need and work with them to amend it. Therefore, we need to empower our teams to provide reasonable and immediate solutions so they may provide a positive service recovery.

Roles and Goals

5 Ps = Proper Planning Prevents Poor Performance.
- LARRY STUART HOSPITALITY

The key to training any incoming team member is to be sure he or she understands our expectations up front—both business culture and performance expectations. It's also important to lay out the consequences for failure to comply with company culture, policy, and job performance fulfillment. We want to discuss expectations and be sure our training structure is very clear. When this is done, there is no excuse for anyone's failure—team member or trainer. We also need to have both sign off on the completed training.

While setting expectations, allow team members to ask questions up front. Alongside sharing what we expect of our team members, the spirit of hospitality would allow the team members to share their expectations with us, the leaders. What can we do to make their learning experience valuable? That would be a key question to ask. Since everyone learns differently, listening to their answers would give us a great clue as to how they will best retain the material we are sharing with them. Some may learn better by watching videos, while others may learn better from experiencing the actual work (i.e. shadowing another team member or hands-on application of their skills). We want our team to understand how working together allows the entire guest experience to flow seamlessly, and properly educating them is going to be our primary goal in order to make that happen. Training, training, training is key.

The first thing our team members will need is clarity of their responsibilities and duties. We need to be sure they understand what they are required to do. The key ingredient in setting expectations is humility. As servant leaders, we need to know how to do every task—menial or not—we are going to require our team members to perform. We need to lead by example. When a member of the team sees we are willing to get down on our knees and clean a toilet, they recognize that they are on a fair playing field. We set expectations, but we also make them achievable.

Some of these duties are simple, while others are more complex. No matter what position the team member holds, there are four key things we must train our team to do immediately.

1. We expect of our team members to greet our guests with eye contact and a sincere smile upon their arrival. Every time our team members see a guest, they should smile and offer an appropriate hospitality comment. They need to speak to every guest in a friendly, enthusiastic, and courteous manner.
2. We also expect them to know our guests by name. If they are unsure of the guest's name, we encourage them to check the name on their credit card, reservation, or by chance their name tag. If the guest is a walk in, have the crew member record their name on the reservations sheet or make a personal note on their account.
3. The staff should be able to answer guests' questions and requests both quickly and efficiently. If they cannot answer, then they need to take the personal responsibility to get the answers as soon as possible. They should not put off finding the answer. It should be done immediately, so as not to forget the task at hand.
4. We also expect them to anticipate a guest's need and to resolve the guest's challenges effectively and efficiently. Staff should know company policy when handling a disgruntled guest, but they

should also have the ability and freedom to find an acceptable solution and implement it immediately, without having to clear it with management, providing it's a reasonable request.

We want to make a difference in our guests' lives by being different—set apart from the rest. The Outback Steakhouse, Ritz Carlton, Belmond Hotels, Southwest Airlines, and Chick-fil-A are fantastic examples of guest service initiative done right. The guest is greeted as soon as they make eye contact with a team member. When the guest's request is acknowledged, so is their name. The guest is not a number in line or the next buck coming through the door. Instead, they are an appreciated relationship with that brand. They're invited into the hotel, airline, or restaurant as if being invited into a home. Leaders and team members can be found wandering the store to check on guests while offering service to the max.

When everyone knows their appropriate role and the tasks that go with it, the work flows smoothly. Without direction, they're likely to stand around wondering what to do, which costs time, money, and successful team performance. Training team members helps to lessen this idleness during the work day. Another key training item is to be sure the team members know what they can do during "down time." Many may not realize they can activate room keys, pick up the trash from under the restaurant tables, or do a sweep of the aisles on the plane to be sure the previous passengers didn't leave anything behind. This should all be included in the training to fulfill their positions well.

Now let's talk about goals. It's important that we not only have daily goals for our team members, but that we also have them for ourselves. Motivation is defined as "an incentive to act." Self-motivation isn't always easily achieved, but there are ways to get motivation going. A little motivation can go a long way in creating excitement and energy to direct toward your work, guests, and fellow staff members. The result? Content staff members and guests. And a happier you!

To be self-motivated, we need a daily vision for ourselves. The first step is to set a long-term goal or vision to strive for. For some it may be to retire or become supervisor/leader. For others, it may be to change careers or work in the same field for another company. Some may only wish to be doing exactly what they're doing today. Long-term goals are important because they give us something to dream about, to hope for, and to shoot for achieving. These make what we do every day—the menial tasks—seem worth it.

Then, we need to set achievable short-term goals. Having daily goals will assist you in being focused on your final vision. If you are able to do what you set out to do daily, you'll have motivation to come in tomorrow and accomplish more. If you over-extend your daily goals, you'll constantly be trying to achieve what you carried over from the day before, never finishing anything. The key to goal setting is to keep your eye on your vision and strive daily to reach that goal, one achievable step at a time.

These goals can be either team oriented, such as improving our bottom line by reaching three attainable short-term objectives. Or, they can be individualized to team members or leaders. These types of goals may improve the work flow process or help a team member reach a new level of their career performance.

Flexibility:

In the hospitality industry, we need to be flexible with people—both those who work with us and those we serve. People are people. We come with our strengths, weaknesses, merits, and faults. We have our good days and our challenging days. Not everyone is going to be nice with us. How we receive and respond to those who are having a challenging day or simply have a negative or selfish attitude toward any moment in life is going to make or break our service.

We strengthen our personal skill sets in how to serve people by being flexible. If it's our way or the highway and we never learn to be flexible, how will we ever learn from the experience? Sure, learning happens best when the experience is a positive one, but we miss out on so much when we don't look to grow through our negative experiences. At the least, we can learn what we don't want to do to others, because we didn't enjoy it when someone else did the same to us. Being flexible in situations that arise will train us how to best respond—and what not to repeat with future guests.

Keep in mind, flexibility is going to be different for each of us. Younger adults don't always understand taking the high road or the basic golden rule of putting others first, whereas someone with more maturity and experience would. We must train our team members to sustain a greater commitment to the spirit of hospitality. In the end, that commitment will wow more guests, build our brand, and increase the team member's personal income.

Optimum Show

One of the reasons I was invited to design, develop, and operate the Walt Disney World Dolphin was because of my experience in the entertainment industry. Octavio Gomez knew the restaurants needed to go above and beyond normal operations, so he brought me to our general manager, Michael Welly. This was Disney. And Disney is all about entertaining their guests. People want to enjoy their time when they come to our restaurant to dine or stay at our hotel while they're on vacation. When presenting the spirit of hospitality, it's always a great idea to employ showmanship. Use drama to create a positive environment. Greet others with enthusiasm. Use an invitation, language, and vocal tones that promote interaction, enjoyment, and happiness. Invite your guests and families to play.

The second facet of showmanship is product knowledge. Product knowledge training is essential to gain guest trust. Guests aren't likely to trust a server who hasn't experienced the entire menu and has to check on answers to guests' questions. What if a guest at your hotel needs a recommendation? Or what if they love the mattress they've slept on and want to know where to get one? Product knowledge is essential and necessary for providing guests with immediate responses to their questions.

Product knowledge is also essential for the upsell. If we don't know what products we're serving, there's no way to perform. For example, we can offer someone who orders steak an addition of shrimp, taking their turf to surf and turf. If we don't naturally order surf and turf, we may not realize we can sell the food items in that way. What about someone who declines dessert? If we understand upselling, we know we don't have to offer a party of four individual desserts. We can recommend one serving of the dessert of the day—or our favorite from the menu—with four forks or spoons so everyone at the table can share it. Now our guests don't feel as if they've been manipulated into spending the extra cash on dessert. They've been offered a chance to partake of it without killing their budget, and they now know we care about their checkbook as much as they do.

Another key component of the upsell is food pairings—knowing what tastes good with the other items on our menu and which drinks will draw out their flavors. This is why we suggest wines with food. The experience becomes even greater when we are able to make these recommendations. We should also know all, not just some, of the products our bar serves. Sometimes a guest may request an alcoholic beverage our bar doesn't carry. Knowing how to offer the product from the top shelf in place of the bottom shelf will produce an appreciated upsell, as long as we let the guest know the cost up front. Never be afraid to let the guest know what they're going to spend. They should always have the option of refusing it.

Granted, the upsell is not only limited to the restaurant business. Hotels upsell rooms. Airlines offer business and first-class seats. The key is to know the benefits and features of each of the items or services we offer in order to successfully upsell.

Showmanship is also the art of giving products personality. Present an idea or product with pizzazz. Personalize the products we sell. It's not simply a bag of popcorn; it's selling "hot, fresh popcorn." It's not the steak at Ruth's Chris Steak House, "it's the sizzle that sells." When we bring the character and personality of an individual together with the character and personality of the product, we have showmanship. If products can't qualify as part of our theme and personality, we shouldn't sell them. Showmanship only works with the products we believe in. Not happy selling a product? Don't. Find something else to sell. It's wise to offer our guests our personal guarantee that we are responsible for our products and services. If someone isn't pleased, honor them as a guest and prove our personal guarantee by removing the item from their check.[10]

Showmanship isn't always appropriate. Sometimes guests don't want to play. They want professional, invisible, accurate service—nothing more, nothing less. Smart, savvy servers know that the show should never interfere with or take precedence over the sequence of service itself. In some cases, the show is the transaction. These are the situations when the guest is paying for a good time. It's important to note that paying for a good time isn't necessarily the same as wanting to participate personally. The guest doesn't want to be the volunteer who enters the stage. They'd rather sit back and enjoy the show. Remember, our guests are paying for an experience that should be driven by their requirement, not ours. We need to dignify them by understanding and recognizing the difference between a guest who wants to participate by interacting with the server and one who wishes to be left alone. If we refuse to do so, our reward disappears because we put our own agenda before the guest's.

Sometimes the upsell isn't appropriate either. Not everyone wants to buy more. Yes, they like to be offered dessert and coffee or an after-dinner drink. That is certainly appropriate at all times. However, some people aren't going to want the hotel suite or first-class seat on the plane. Guests don't come to our establishment for the staff member to become the car salesman, always trying to push the deal on them. I was recently charged an extra $3.50 for a bleu cheese-stuffed olive in my martini and nearly gasped when I discovered that charge on my check. I could almost buy an entire jar of bleu cheese-filled olives for that price. Always make sure the guest wants to pay the charge before presenting them with the "extra." Pay attention to their body language. This is another area where our team members need to be trained to recognize and anticipate guests needs—or needlessness.

When we train our staff as entertaining salespeople, they will have a great time performing their jobs, and their morale will increase. When that occurs, their loyalty to the company also increases. Another benefit to training our staff to entertain our guests is that the experience at our establishment will then become an "event" versus a typical dining experience. The guests' expectations will be exceeded, and they will be more likely to share with their friends how much they need to visit us. ROI and growth will be inevitable.

Recognition

People love to be acknowledged, whether for a job well done, their need, or even their presence. There are several aspects of recognition to specify in training.

The first is recognition of someone's presence. This is the welcoming smile and a pleasant "Welcome to …". Our team members also like it when we recognize their presence. It never hurts to address them when they come on site and ask how they're doing. If we don't know it already, we must get their name and address them by it.

The second is to recognize needs, whether they are felt or tangible. If a guest is frowning as a front desk associate tries to find an available room and is running through the description of a room with one queen bed, the guest's frown may point to a need for a king-sized bed or two queens. Or they may prefer the upsell to the suite. Team members need to be able to recognize body language in order to anticipate the expectations of guests and ask if they need assistance, and it's always helpful if leadership is able to recognize the needs of team members in the same manner. Everyone's needs vary depending on job level of training, job tools, communication abilities, expectations, health issues, personal challenges, and so much more. Team members may need a day off to take a sick child or elderly parent to a medical appointment. If a team member appears anxious or down or otherwise off, they will understand we care when we recognize they aren't on their game. Once we've established what the need is, we are then able to properly address it in a professional and compassionate manner. This spirit of hospitality initiative demonstrates how important our team members are to us.

Train team members to go "off script" and connect with clients to exemplify their experience. Many companies have canned responses they train their guest service specialists to use. When we apply the spirit of hospitality to our guest service initiative, our responses should never sound canned, scripted, or rehearsed. These just make guests feel like another number added to our income statement. Allowing team members to actually converse with guests, ask appropriate questions, and provide appropriate answers will strengthen the bond of trust with them. Having a normal conversation with a guest recognizes him or her as a person with individual needs and builds relationship and morale.

Time Management

Proper time management is key to productivity, no matter what position we're responsible for. Without time management, tasks fall to the wayside and don't get accomplished. It's important to train our team members to manage their time in a way that gets the job done and done well.

Often, when we think of time management, we think of it on the job. How can we better manage our working hours in order to accomplish more in a day? Have you ever considered it in light of saving from distractions on the job? Hyatt Hotels Corporation offers their housekeeping a flextime program. Room attendants are allowed to begin or end their shift when it's convenient for them, and as long as the attendant finishes their duties within their shift, they are paid the full eight hours, even if they clock out early.[11]

There are a few things this does:

1. It frees them to schedule appointments as needed and not have to fit them into a specific time slot such as during busy after-hours or weekends. Some people schedule all of the family's appointments for a specific day of the week once a month and take that day off. This saves a team member from inconsistency in their work hours, allowing for a regular workflow.
2. It allows them to focus on their job instead of focusing on the doctor's appointment, oil change, or grocery run they need to

make. Once those things are taken care of, their attention shifts to the task at hand.

3. It empowers them to set their schedule. Knowing the rooms need to be cleaned or turned over by 3:00 check-in time, they'll know ahead of time when they need to be there for that particular day's work. It also allows them to leave earlier if they accomplish their tasks in less than eight hours.

Once we've established a schedule with our team members, we need to focus on training them in time management regarding handling those tasks at work. Efficiency is what all of this comes down to. One of the best ways to be efficient is to learn to save steps. I'm not talking about skipping steps in order to get somewhere faster. Shortcuts rarely work in business. What I'm talking about is making sure we have all the tools we need in order to clean a room so we aren't running back and forth between the rooms or floors and the supply closet or laundry room.

Training our team members to think ahead, be proactive instead of reactive, and prep ahead will increase work flow and decrease mistakes, dropped plates, and cost on the back end. When we properly manage our time, we make room to exceed our guests' expectations.

Make Learning Fun

We can't expect our team members to be perfect and know how to do it all the moment we hire them. Training is an important tool in shaping our team into a well-oiled, functioning machine. Patience and kindness are key during the training process. Lessons are better, more quickly learned when given by a gentle spirit with a kind tongue. No one learns well when their leader is a drill sergeant. Yelling, rolling our eyes, and acting disgusted will not produce a crew member eager to get to work for us. We must remember to be patient with those we're called to lead. We must persevere through time and adversity, remembering to be empathic and encouraging. None of us are perfect, nor will we get it right all of the time.

I served as an adjunct professor of hospitality at Valencia College in Orlando, Florida. The position required a lot of work for hardly any compensation. If money were my motive for teaching, I never would have taken the position. My motive was to positively affect as many students as I could over the five-year period I served in that capacity. The key thing I did to win the students' attention and participation was to create a fun, hands-on-learning atmosphere. I encouraged my students to engage, make mistakes, and take risks. In return, the students would charge my desk, full of enthusiasm, asking questions and hoping for positive reinforcement when they succeeded. Sometimes, they asked for recommendations concerning their career paths. Nothing beats the joy of seeing a student grasp a concept based on what you've taught them. I would encourage you to make learning fun for your team members every day in every way. Building enthusiasm will bond team members and create positive memories for our staff and the guests who will experience their guest service delivery.

Follow Up

Winning is all about being proactive, not reactive.
– **LARRY STUART HOSPITALITY**

We can't have a spirit of hospitality and hold people responsible for their attitudes, words, and actions without understanding and accountability. As our new hires complete training and become fully functioning members of our team, we need to follow up with them. And then we need to continue doing so throughout their career with our company.

Our team as a whole and as individuals will have much better overall performance if we as leaders implemented planning, daily coaching, and evaluations. Doing so will develop a team that thrives. In this section, we're going to focus on evaluation and redirection.

We want to be proactive on the front end. Having a five-step leadership process in place will result in providing a leadership model, growth, and direction for our team members.

1. **Tell with structure, focus, and enthusiasm.** When training our team members, we need to provide clarity, as mentioned earlier in this chapter. Doing so with enthusiasm will encourage them to enjoy the process and build a positive attitude toward their responsibilities and successful work efforts.

2. **Show through positive and professional example.** We must be willing to first do what we expect our team members to do, and we need to do so with class and professionalism.

3. **Let the team member practice in a relaxed environment.** It's stressful enough for someone walking into a new position at a potentially new company. When our environment is relaxed and allows for the team member to learn in a safe, encouraging environment, they are more likely to receive whatever correction we may need to bring. It also encourages learning. It's difficult to retain information when someone is standing over our shoulder, breathing down our neck, and barking orders. Let your team practice their new skills in a relaxed, comfortable environment. Rather than bringing them in to serve tables for the first time during lunch hour, start them mid-morning or mid-afternoon. Allow them to get the hang of it before pushing them into the busiest time of day, which will only overwhelm them.

4. **Observe performance with a supporting attitude of encouragement.** When our team members know that we're paying attention to what they're doing and saying and that we're available to help them as needed, they understand we support them and aren't merely looking for them to fail. Promoting their success is key to promoting a positive work attitude and job productivity.

5. **Praise progress and/or redirect an action.** Encourage correction of mistakes by applauding what they've done correctly and

then discussing how to correct what's wrong. Use the sandwich method. Applause-Redirect-Applause. This is the best way to bring correction or redirection and encourages our team members to avoid mistakes in the future.

The road to the spirit of hospitality is not without its challenges and shortfalls. We're all human. We all make mistakes. And there will come a time when a team member is going to need correction. They key is to remember that correction should always be done with care and kindness. It should never include shame, blame, or pain. Those will only stunt growth, not promote it. But we shouldn't avoid correcting issues that need to be resolved. Doing so will help our team members find their greatest heights.

One thing to consider is that we may have the right message but the wrong delivery. My friend and fellow customer service leader, Ron Bellomo, points out that it's easy to find someone doing something wrong. We look for people doing the wrong thing instead of finding someone doing the right thing. When we find that team member or group of team members who are doing what they were asked to do, we should thank them in front of everyone so that the next time, the people who haven't responded to our direction will respond. Why does this work? Because they'll want to be acknowledged for their productivity too.

Sometimes correction isn't enough. If a team member is struggling with any area of their job performance, whether using a skill, developing a positive attitude, smiling, or any other number of aspects of work, we may need to provide them with more training. Sometimes people don't grasp the skill set on the first try. Sometimes they require more practice. It's our job to recognize that need and set up the training to develop that skill set.

Other times, our team members may learn better through a mentorship program. At the heart of a good leader is someone who desires to share what they know. We can't be in a business of one. We must be about the business of training those future leaders around us and allowing them opportunities for advancement. We do this by mentoring, supporting, and guiding our fellow team members. When a leader recognizes a gift or talent in a team member, we should be ready and willing to draw it out of them without fear of takeover. In business, this would be a welcoming way to encourage and grow new leadership, demonstrating the spirit of hospitality.

Southwest Airlines has a program called "Cohearts." Longer-term team members take new hires under their wings for six months.[12] This allows a new team member to learn from someone who already has the experience they'll need to gain. Leaders can also rest a little easier knowing that they have someone who can answer the new hires' questions as they arise, rather than having to do so themselves. This solution protects leadership from consistent interruptions throughout their work day, improving work flow for everyone.

It's Important to Invest in Training

If you've watched the news in the past few years, you've seen the reports about a handful of airlines and their lack of guest service skills. When I asked my friend, Ron Brennan, about it, he had an interesting fact to share. Unfortunately, the airlines are relying more on technology to train their personnel than leaders—people—in the industry. This lack of human interaction during training is causing the subsequent lack of guest service and proper responses to issues that arise during flights.

There was a time when the airline industry proudly competed by providing proper service principles. Now we compete with price and deliver service with computers, phone-loop recordings, slogans, and platitudes. As they once did, the airline industry no longer trains their staff with guest service principles, nor do they conduct recurrent training on the subject. Most non-technical training is done via CBT (Computer-based Training), not by people. The human element—the spirit of hospitality—is missing. Further, the airline industry no longer takes into account the "guests need to be understood" ethic. This results in crew members forgetting to treat passengers as individuals who have particular needs.

As a result, ground and inflight crews are more militant and regimented since Sept. 11, 2001. Moreover, DOT/FAA regulations are far more familiar to guest service personnel than the airlines' guest service policies, as these regulations are highly stressed. The problem is they are driven into our personnel without the training as how to best apply these measures. Today, the culture of airline personnel is that they see themselves as "Enforcers." They feel enabled and justified by Federal Security FARs, along with corporate policy. Common sense is also not so common. Left to their own devices, the "Enforcer" attitude has proliferated. Ron has actually seen where some, not all, are looking for trouble and challenging passengers at large. He sees no apparent conflict resolution training whatsoever.

To be fair, many—particularly flight attendants—are fearful beyond practical reason. It's should not be "What you are doing?" but rather, "How are you practicing safe security?" Be vigilant, not a vigilante. This holds true especially for all operational, middle-leadership decision makers right on down to the day-to-day operating crew members.

A matrix check list and training of who, what, and how to do is sorely missing. This is not hard stuff, but it does take follow up and energy. Do it! Guest-service-failures alarm bells and sirens are sounding off. With proper training, that issue of the mom bringing her stroller onto the plane could have been easily resolved and not rise to an appalling nationally exposed service failure. Reset and treat people with respect. Train, train, and train.

Training Must Be Ongoing

One dollar spent on training will save you three in advertising. The better the guest service is, the more likely a guest will be to spread the word about their incredible experience they had at your establishment. The only way to improve guest service is through consistent training of our team members, which will result in providing consistent products and services.

Learning is a lifelong process. Things change every day. Fads come and go. Menus have items added or deleted. Codes get updated. It's important for our team to know when something has changed that will affect them. Just as we mentioned earlier that we need to know our quality service standards and products well, we need to update the team each time there's a service delivery or product change. We can't tell them once and expect it to be that way forever. It's unrealistic to do so. Keep the team updated so they may consistently serve the guest with current information.

Our most valuable asset is our internal guest. Investing in them and committing to their development, not just another training program, should be a top priority. Investing in our team members shows them they are important as human beings and not just a slave to our operation and their job. Our investment starts with our training programs, but it shouldn't stop there. Marriott International, Inc. understands this. Their founding principle says that associates who are well taken care of will take good care of guests. First, they do their best to make their team members feel like family, offering time off when needed, massage therapy, vehicle maintenance, and personal travel service. But, they don't stop there. They strive to celebrate one another's successes, implementing several development programs for their team members and offering a variety of awards that honor those who strive for excellence in their work life.

How does all of this affect their turnover? One team member stated that their founding principle is one of the perks of working for them. "This is why it's so hard to leave ... The benefits and the welcome wherever you go makes you feel like family, which is what keeps me."[13] When we focus on developing our team members' character and invest in improving their lives, they will be more likely to remain committed to serving others and working for our company, possibly for life.

TAKEOUT:

Guests don't want automated, robotic service. In order to provide excellent, personalized customer service, we must PERFORM when training our internal guests to serve our external guests. Remember, PERFORM:

- ▶ Purpose
- ▶ Empathy
- ▶ Roles and Goals
- ▶ Flexibility
- ▶ Optimum Show
- ▶ Recognition
- ▶ Morale

We were created to be part of a team, a family.
There is far greater strength in numbers.
Alone, I can only do so much.
Together, we can change the world.
LARRY STUART HOSPITALITY

5

T.E.A.M. – Together Everyone Achieves More

Teamwork is the ability to work together toward a common vision.
It is the fuel that allows common people to attain uncommon results.
– ANDREW CARNEGIE

Teamwork is a cooperative effort by the members of a team to achieve a common goal. The key words in the definition are *cooperative effort*. Independence fails us when we forget we're part of a team working toward one common goal for one common cause. In the hospitality business, that goal would be serving both our internal and external guests with a spirit of hospitality. Without the support of the entire group, no team can long endure.

Chefs quickly learn that no one member of the kitchen team can be the star of every dish or restaurant. Most moments of glory are built upon a long series of trial and error, each victory achieved by commitment and determination to combine the ingredients until they create the perfect dish. Without a T.E.A.M. (Together Everyone Achieves More) mentality, we'll always be limited to performing menial individual tasks that will never be as rewarding as winning the coveted Michelin Stars. But in order to win, we must be committed to work as a unified front. And that starts with servant leadership.

Servant Leadership

Understanding authority is the key to leadership. As leaders, we need to recognize that we not only have authority over those who work as members of our team, but that we too answer to someone, whether it's a board of directors, corporate, or God. I am under authority. I am in authority. Recognizing this authority reminds us that we need to operate in compassion, empathy, and respect for those over us and those working beside us. We also need to be well aware of the language we're using when discussing matters of business and fellow workers. Are we speaking positive, respectful words? Are we operating in a spirit of hospitality? Or are we tearing down what someone else has worked so hard to build? Servant leaders know how to be respectful and encourage growth.

- ▸ **Servant leaders are selfless.** This requires putting others first, whether we're talking about accomplishing what our direct supervisor is asking of us or we are mentoring a team member or handling a guest's request. Our own desire to hide at our desk will need to come second to the team's need for help on the floor because there's a convention checking in, there are too many cars to park at once, housekeeping doesn't have rooms prepared because people are arriving early, and technology is acting up. Leaders should not be prideful, thinking they are the most important person on their team. Rather, they should always put their fellow teammates and guests before themselves. We need to be examples of selflessness. Our guests will notice when a leader takes the floor to make sure all is well and they are comfortable while they wait to be checked into their rooms.
- ▸ **Servant leaders are strategists who lead by example and are always willing to go before their team members.** As a servant leader, we must be willing to lay down our desk work and come alongside our team members. We must know the proper way to do all of the tasks we ask others to do, and we must be willing to do them if someone calls in sick and we end up short handed.

Team members will be far more likely to follow a leader who isn't afraid to roll up their sleeves and join the crew during the dinner rush over someone who sits behind a closed door in the name of checking on or updating their administrative requirements.

▸ **Servant leaders plan out the necessary steps to meet a goal.** Part of strategizing is knowing how to get from concept to final product. It's also knowing how to create a work flow that sees a guest from making a reservation to pulling up to the curb to entering the hotel and checking in to getting into their room to enjoying their stay to checking out—and doing so successfully. When a servant leader appropriately plans for these things, the team can successfully execute their individual roles until the task is accomplished.

▸ **Servant leaders are proactive.** While working at the Statler Hotel at Cornell University, I learned to be a team player. Whether I was cooking in the kitchen, serving in the restaurant, or checking in guests at the front desk, I understood that in order for the establishment to function well, I needed to work well with others. While we each have our various, individual job functions in the hospitality industry, all of our positions are interrelated. If the housekeepers don't have the rooms clean, the front desk agents can't check in guests on time. If the front desk can't check in guests, the guest becomes irritated. How many times have you had a guest enter your establishment and ask if they could check in early because they have someplace they need to be at three in the afternoon? Imagine the same guest showing up for their three o'clock check in and the room not being ready. The hotel staff's error may end up costing the guest a major business deal when they show up late for their dinner meeting because the room wasn't ready for them.

Granted, everyone has their days. Maybe the front desk clerk just found out his grandfather passed away and was distracted when the client called and requested an early check in, so he forgot to write it down on the housekeeper's schedule. Not knowing about the early check in, the housekeeper can't be blamed for the room being dirty at three in the afternoon during a week of solid bookings. When life happens, we have to find a way to work around it so our team can continue to operate in a seamless manner. Maybe we need to give the front desk clerk the afternoon off so nothing more is overlooked. Or, maybe we need to bring in an extra housekeeper when the hotel is booked solid. Leaders need to be great communicators, "inspecting—not expecting," while being proactive, providing for their team's success.

Know Your Team Members

To build a team, you must first understand who your players really are. When I was regional director of food and beverage at Loews Hotels at Universal Studios in Florida, I hired Adnan Bizri to be the executive director of food and beverage at the Portofino Bay Hotel. My first objective was to work to build a relationship with him. We began to meet daily. During that time, we discussed our operating philosophies, past experiences, hospitality values, leadership styles, and our thoughts on the hotel. Throughout the six months I was focusing on building this relationship, we hired and trained our opening team, designed and developed restaurants and lounges, provided culinary and beverage direction, procured our equipment, and enjoyed the pleasure of watching our guests' expectations being exceeded. As the relationship developed, we bonded and a level of trust formed between us. I took the time to find out what made him tick—his passions, strengths, and weaknesses. Because I got to know him and his personality, he wasn't at arm's length from me as just another crew member. I could talk with him on a personal level. Knowing who he was as a person allowed me to support, empower, and encourage him toward his future success.

It only takes leadership a few extra moments in their day to come alongside a team member and show him that he matters to him, not just as a team member of the company, but as an individual who happened to be a part of the team. Why is this important? Bonding naturally occurs when you know your fellow teammates. And when bonding occurs, the team functions in unity, because the members genuinely care about one another.

Everyone Plays a Part

Everyone wants to feel like they are a part of something, like they have a larger purpose and are part of a bigger, more magnificent plan. When we treat our team members like they're part of a larger picture and not just their job description, they are more likely to be encouraged to participate, take ownership in, and stay on with our company.

By looking at our team members as internal guests, we recognize they are individuals with their own needs and desires and talents and skills, and we acknowledge them as such. Being part of a team is where we can all come together, each with our individuality, in the warm, secret place where the spirit of hospitality can be shared by those who best understand its language.

In 1976, I rented an apartment from a landlord named Mary. Mary's seamstress abilities rivaled that of Betsey Ross's. She created the most colorful, soft, unique quilts I've ever seen. Each one had its own personality, and each told its own story. They also served the purpose they were created for—keeping me warm on chilly Kansas City winter nights. I loved wrapping up in her quilt and lying next to the fireplace while watching television. But Mary wasn't the only one involved in the quilt-making process.

Mary had a team of seamstresses, all equally talented, working alongside her to create those beautiful quilts. Nettie, Bea, and Lula all had a particular purpose in that process. Nettie cut patches of material. Bea stitched the patches together, and Lula prepared the cotton padding that would be sown in between the quilt and its back cover. Mary directed the team, making sure they were all on point to accomplish the end goal of producing a beautiful piece of artwork.

Producing a quilt is no easy task. It took Mary and her team two to three weeks to complete one quilt. Before they could even begin the cutting and sewing process, they had to design the pattern, purchase the materials, and prepare for the labor ahead of them. When they worked together, they built something beautiful that would last for generations.

Each team member has a unique purpose to serve within our chosen industry. From an outside perspective, what we do may look a mess as someone observes our piles of thread, material scraps, and tools scattered about. But when we pull all that together, each one doing his or her assigned position with excellence, we produce something we can be proud of.

Balancing the System

No matter what industry we work in, no position is more important than any other position. Without one position, the system isn't balanced and doesn't work. When I interned with "Mr. Bodo" Von Alvensleben at the Elbow Beach Hotel in Bermuda, we were faced with a three-week industry strike. Every one of the executive leaders performed every job in the hotel. One hundred and twenty-five team members typically held those positions, and twenty-one of us had to fill the void the strike had left. We started at 4:00 a.m., cooking and serving breakfast, meeting our guests' needs, turning over and freshening the rooms, maintaining the building, cooking and serving lunch and dinner, checking in new guests and checking out those whose stay had ended. I was twenty when I had this experience, and it added to the foundation for my spirit of hospitality. Working under pressure will always change and refine us, hopefully for the better.

As evidenced above, it doesn't matter if the missing person is at the top of the corporate ladder or the bottom. Without each position filled and functioning at its best capacity, the system won't work. Leaders need to recognize that they are no better than the person doing the least job at the company. Everyone is equally important. It takes a humble leader to recognize this and set a company culture where everyone feels needed and important.

From the day they are hired, our staff members should understand they are now part of a team. And not just any team, but a united front. Working together isn't always easy, but none of the best things in life come easily. It requires focus, hard work, and patience. As well as brotherly love. We must learn to give up some of our personal control, trust and depend on others to do their part, compromise when disagreements arise, be considerate of one another and willing to put others before ourselves. We should consistently look for opportunities to make someone's day by offering compassion, listening, and responding with respect. We are part of a team of many capable individuals. Like a working body, every member has its function. Without one, the system fails. When all are doing their part, the system runs smoothly, allowing the body to live at its fullest potential. We are not in business for ourselves. We depend on our fellow team members and colleagues, and they depend on us. Be friendly and helpful. If we are, others will be friendly and helpful to us. We reap what we sow. People are more likely to want to serve our vision for the company if they know they're important and appreciated. When team members feel as though we care about them, they'll care about their work.

TAKEOUT:

▶ Ultimately, our business is owned by the staff who serve the guests. Without them, we wouldn't have commerce and eventually, we wouldn't have an establishment.

▶ When a service team can come together and work to help each other, the workflow functions well and the guests are consistently happy.

▶ It's up to us as servant leaders to draw the team together, creating a healthy work environment not only for our internal guests, but so that we can serve our external guests with a fully functioning spirit of hospitality.

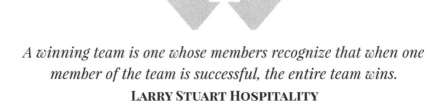

A winning team is one whose members recognize that when one member of the team is successful, the entire team wins.
LARRY STUART HOSPITALITY

6

Unity

Individual commitment to a group effort—that is what makes a team work, a company work, a society work, a civilization work.
– Vince Lombardi

In order to operate in unity, all members of the team, leadership included, need to operate with a likeminded approach. We have to, as individuals, choose to work with a servant's heart. How well everything comes together depends entirely upon how well we execute our responsibilities and how those responsibilities work in unity to create the entire guest service experience. We yield our personal will, committing to come together as a team. When every member is responsibly fulfilling their position, business runs smoothly and guests are happy. As soon as one member fails to perform their duty or does so without care of how well it's done, the ebb and flow changes, sometimes with disastrous results.

I had planned to surprise my god parents while we were on a summer cruise to Bermuda. During the booking process, I specifically told the cruise representative how important it was for eight of us to be sitting together during our meal period. He confirmed our dining reservations had been merged. I was finally going to provide them with the surprise of their lives.

After arriving on the cruise ship, we discovered that our dining reservations were all over the place, which thwarted my plan to surprise our family members. I immediately went to meet the leader of guest services and explained our dilemma. What the leader stated up front is that lot of what is processed at Miami headquarters doesn't transfer to the ship. After being inconvenienced for over three hours, the miscommunication between shore side and the ship was corrected to the best of their ability. After paying thousands of dollars, I found this sad and inexcusable. Although the cruise line provided a solution of restitution, they should have never provided details regarding the fragmented lack of communication within their operations. In the end, our family made the cruise a good one, but what we experienced in their failures created a negative perception of their brand in my mind.

Unity in the team starts with us, the servant leaders. We are the mortar that holds the foundation together. If we don't walk in unity, we can't expect our team members to follow suit. In order to avoid a disaster like the one I just mentioned, we need to walk the walk and set the example for others to follow.

Barriers to Unity

The ability to seamlessly fit into a team environment where we work together in harmony for the greater good of our guests isn't as easy as one would expect. Anything can get in the way of like-mindedness, including—but not limited to—our own personalities, any variety of circumstances, or even the business atmosphere.

1. **Individuality Clash:** Everyone on the team is unique, from leaders all the way down to the sanitation engineer or the housekeeper. We have our own personalities, our own life experiences, and our own way of seeing things. Sometimes these aspects of our individuality don't work well with one another. This can lead to dissension among the ranks, back biting, gossiping, and a lack of productivity across departments. We don't only interact with our team members, either. Throw a disgruntled guest in the mix, and things can quickly go south if our team isn't unified.

2. **The Gang's All Here:** Working together is the important thing. Don't permit team members to be drawn into cliques or special groups who set themselves apart from the other team members. We're not in high school anymore. We need to get beyond a mindset of everyone out for themselves or being more important than someone else. Again, none of us is more special than the other, and each of our roles is important to the workflow. Cliques promote exclusion. We want everyone on our staff to be all in.

3. **Competition:** Another sure way to develop a losing formula is to create an environment in which team members compete with one another. This leaves each member of the team fighting for their own survival. The weak links fail, as their spirits are tested to the very core. We aren't in business to achieve high sales and five-star ratings at the cost of our team, causing them to lose heart, become ill from the stress we've placed on them, or forcing them to quit. A house divided against itself will fall, and a team divided against one another will fail.

Teams that are built to last have all the right ingredients, the most important being the spirit of hospitality—character. That's the core value that will protect your team culture from eroding away when pride, greed, envy, and other power-hungry diseases threaten its life. When all members give their best in every situation, whether they are carrying the ball or clearing the way for someone else, the team wins and so does each member, including the executive leadership. If we focus on serving with a spirit of hospitality, we will always come out on top.

Togetherness Is Best

No one wants to work with someone who causes consistent conflict. Do we have to always agree on everything? Not necessarily. But we should always agree on the important things, like our company values, and be aware that we're all working toward the same vision. This is the concept of like-mindedness. To establish a team that works in unity, we must consistently work to promote it.

▸ **Establish Values.** From the beginning, we need to establish value sets for the individual, the department, and the company. Everyone who works under our corporate banner should know the common points of these value sets and how they're related to what we do and how we do it. Without these values, everyone is left to their own, and not everyone we hire may share our personal or corporate morality. This is why it's so incredibly important to hire people who possess the spirit of hospitality and train the skills they need so they can serve our guests in a manner that will exceed their expectations. Build a successful team by setting a firm foundation of company values. Then be sure those values flow to the various departments and individuals doing the work in those departments.

▸ **Review Goals.** This also needs to be done at a personal level, a departmental level, and company-wide. Everyone in the company needs to have a goal to achieve. This provides direction, as well as communicating that even as individuals, we all interact to reach goals as a whole. We work together to provide the entire experience our guests will encounter when they visit our facilities.

▸ **Relate the Values to the Goals.** This will develop a behavior or performance to what the department and each person in the department must do to satisfy the goals and be consistent with values. This also explains why we do what we do in the way we do it. When someone understands why their task is important and what they are accomplishing by fulfilling their obligation, they contribute to the overall value of the guest experience. In 1955, a week after Disneyland opened, an interviewer was touring the park and mentioned to Walt Disney that it would never stay clean. Walt responded that it would because "people are going to be embarrassed to throw anything on the ground." Since then,

Disney's cast members have been taught that their first rule is "We create happiness," and the second rule is "Everyone picks up trash."[14] Every cast member values cleanliness, because they uphold the values of the Disney company. Their goal is a positive, wow-factor guest experience. And when team members care that much about the minor details of the day-to-day operations of the company, they care enough to provide it.

▶ **Demonstrate Team Relations.** We must have a vision of where we want to be and how we get from where we are now to where we want to go. Without vision, people have no idea what they are working toward. When this happens, team performance, guest satisfaction, and ROI remain stagnant, if they don't fail. Our team members need to know what impact they make by fulfilling and exceeding their position's responsibilities. They need to understand that they, as individuals, are valuable not only for their personal success, but also for their team's success and the company's success as we serve the guests who walk through our doors. Everyone needs to know what the team must do and what each member is responsible for in order to make that happen. Again, if further training or redirection is required, it will only improve the team and their success to put a member or multiple members through that training. The team needs to relate well with one another in their various functions in order to successfully operate in unity.

Team building is the best investment you'll ever make.
– LARRY STUART HOSPITALITY

Trust

Building trust with our team members is important for promoting unity on the team. How do we build trust with our spouses, children, neighbors, and other people we relate with? It all comes down to character. If we have solid, golden character, we always keep our word. Our yes is yes. Our no is no. If I'm leading people in a business, they need to know my word is golden. I will do what I say I'm going to do. The minute we compromise our character, it all comes down to numbers. Leaders without character will only do what's required to line their pockets, and if that's you, your team members will automatically assume you don't care one iota about them.

One team member at a local casual restaurant talked with me about her leaders. One was obviously supportive of the team while the other was more concerned with the bottom line. For example, a guest requested almond milk with her oatmeal. The food deliverer went to give her an adequate amount of milk when the person in charge took it from her and forced her to give the guest a takeout-condiment-sized container of the milk. Would it really cost the restaurant that much more to serve their guest? No. Fortunately, the guest didn't cry over spilled milk. But she could have. And the restaurant's character could have been attacked online via a negative review. All it takes is one tweet to a wide audience for our business to receive a negative impression. And our team members can usually recognize our personal greed as sloppy leaders without much effort. As servant leaders, we must remember that others are watching us, even when we think they aren't. And if our internal guest knows we care so little for an external guest, they'll know they're not at the top of our priority list either.

Let's contrast the casual dining leadership with my local Trader Joe's leader, Captain Jim. Every chance I get, I try to say hello to Captain Jim when I'm in the store. This particular afternoon, I couldn't find him so I thought he wasn't there. Imagine my delight when I discovered he was at the front of the store, running a register. That is a servant leader. That builds trust. When the leadership is on the floor working side by side with their people, the team members take note, and doing so builds trust between them and their leaders.

Our team members will perform based on how much we care about them and how much we provide for or nurture them to be successful. Just as I mentioned at the end of the training chapter, the better we care for our internal guests, the better they'll care for our external guests. Without leaders serving the team, there is no team. It becomes segregated, as leadership takes on the attitude of either being in a position or doing something more important than those who are on the front lines, serving our guests. That's not in our best interests or the best interest of the company, because it will lead to increased turnover. And that costs more money.

Barriers to Trust

In order to accomplish things with others, we have to give up some control. For those of us who are perfectionists at heart or Type A personalities, this is difficult. We know that there are ways to do things that work well, but not everyone will do things the way we would. For example, every hotel has standards for how the beds are supposed to be made, how to fold the toilet paper over, and where items are to be placed in the rooms. These are areas where the standard is set. What will not matter as much is the order in which the housekeeper does the tasks required of her position. One may like to knock out the bathroom first and then make the beds and vacuum the floor, while another may prefer to clean the room before moving to the bathroom.

Does that make their system wrong and ours right? Certainly not. This is where we who may be OCD about something need to take a deep breath and note that the task is successfully completed. As long as it isn't going to affect the entire system or doesn't go against company standards, we need to learn the art of compromise. The delivery process should always be standardized, professional, and consistent. But our team should also have the ability to use their creativity and add their unique personality to their presentation. We simply cannot expect everyone to be just like us.

The same concept goes into learning to trust and depending on others. If a team member isn't going to do things the same way we are or to the utmost standard—even if he's met the standard—we as leaders can decide to do the job ourselves rather than delegate. Before doing so, we need to ask ourselves if doing the extra work will interfere with our own to-do list.

It's likely we need to learn to trust our team members to do their jobs and do them well. If we've trained them properly, this shouldn't be a challenge. And if we allow them the opportunity to prove they can successfully use their skills to complete their tasks, not only will it provide them with confidence, it will build our trust and relieve our anxieties, resulting in a stronger operation. We need to give them a chance to prove themselves capable. Servant leaders will come alongside and encourage, only taking further action when a team member has proven they no longer hold the same values as the company and its leadership.

When working as a team, we must always be considerate and put others before ourselves. Never forget that life is most rewarding and meaningful when we join hands, huddle up, fight for and do things together.

TAKEOUT:

- ▸ Without unity, a team will fall apart.
- ▸ It's important for servant leaders to remember there is no "I" in team and come alongside their team members to serve both the internal and external guests.
- ▸ When internal guests trust their leaders, external guests are treated well.

The greatest shot in the arm is encouragement.
LARRY STUART HOSPITALITY

7

Encouragement

Encouragement is like oxygen to the human spirit. Don't forget you're carrying someone else's air. Encourage them; help them breathe.
– JEREMY RIDDLE

Servant leaders are champions. Not only in themselves, but for others. A champion is someone who gets up even when he can't. He has a relentless and enduring spirit. When he gets knocked down, he always brushes himself off and keeps on keeping on. These leaders know how to encourage those around them to get past their challenges and failures and continue to grow. As team leaders and store leaders and CEOs, we must champion our team members.

As humans, we love getting credit when credit is due. We even love taking the credit when we're at the top of the ladder. What we tend to forget is that our success was a team effort. Others were involved in the process, helping meet the goal or gain the award. As servant leaders, we must acknowledge those who helped us reach our achievements. The ladder of success always depends on others helping us up. One day, we're going to pass them as we head back down the corporate ladder toward retirement. It's important to build up others through encouragement and reward so they remember us with honor and respect, not begrudgingly.

We must also be sure that everyone on our team wins, not just some chosen few. Again, success is a team effort. Southwest doesn't turn planes around in twenty minutes without the baggage handlers on the ground. They are as much a part of the airline's success as the pilots in getting the passengers to their destinations in a timely manner. We cannot single out our favorites and forget about the rest. As servant leaders, it's important that our team members all receive accolades for a successful guest service delivery. One cannot succeed without the others. And be sure to praise all who were involved, not just the obvious people.

Don't take all the credit, either. Leaders wouldn't be successes without their team. When the company has achieved a goal or found success, pass on the credit to those who are doing the work behind the scenes. Recognize the hard work they've done to get the company where it is today. Praise the job well done, too. Acknowledging a particular team member who has put forth an A-plus effort and really pulled one for the team demonstrates we recognize exceptional work. It also reminds her fellow team members what accomplishing their tasks merits.

If we had a daily practice of recognizing our team members for their exemplary work, rather than waiting for an annual award ceremony to do so, we would witness a higher team morale, less turnover, and more bottom-line profit. Texas Roadhouse, a fantastic example of this, recognizes their team members' anniversaries and significant achievements consistently throughout the year. They also acknowledge Roadie of the Quarter and then Roadie of the Year. There are leadership awards and the Department of the Year award. The winner of the Managing Partner of the Year Award earns him or herself $25,000, a car, a ring, a silver belt buckle, and a pair of cowboy boots.[15]

As our team members grow in their service experience, it's likely we'll recognize their skill sets. Some may even develop leadership traits. Rather than threatening our position, these talents should be pulled out of the team member and put to excellent use. In today's world, so many are afraid someone is going to usurp their position or take their job or any other number of things. We've become so focused on our own need or fear that we forget the world doesn't revolve around us. Others have needs and fears as well, and it's better to allow everyone to operate in the fullest capacity of their gifts and talents, affording them the best opportunity to succeed in their own right.

One of the ways to do this successfully is to rotate servant leaders, giving everyone a shot at being the head. Hyatt Regency has successfully rotated team members in leadership positions from department to department or hotel to hotel for years. This is a great way for our teams to stay fresh and on top of their game, benefiting not only the leaders but the brand as well. We never know what talent is lying hidden inside of someone until we give them an opportunity to reveal it. By rotating leaders on our team, we allow for a variety of people to draw out the best in others. Maybe we have someone on our team who is excellent at handling the difficult guests. Where one person lacks patience and self-control, another may have it in abundance. Maybe someone else has the talent of calming an irate guest, bringing the person out of their red zone and back into a reasonable state of control. Who wouldn't want that person on the front end, serving as a model leader?

We need to encourage ourselves and our team members to push forward and grow in our areas of weakness and continue to develop our strengths. Encouragement isn't always easy to come by. We all have naysayers in our lives who like to scoff at our latest, greatest ideas and cut us down, telling us we don't have what it takes to achieve anything we've put our minds to do. As bearers of the spirit of hospitality, encouragement should come naturally to us. Every member of our team should walk in it every moment of every day.

Ways to Encourage Others

There are several ways to encourage someone: compliments, singing their praises, bringing a comforting word during a difficult time, coming alongside them as they struggle to improve in an area. These are just a few, but you get the idea. What I'd like to talk about here is the encouragement of reward. In a thankless job, encouragement from a superior at the company goes so much further than the occasional review and possible raise. Many team members want to know they have opportunity for growth and upward movement at the company they're pouring their time and talents into. Let's take a look at how we can successfully encourage our team members to continue improving their performance, attitudes, and overall bring us a return on our investment.

First and foremost, figure out what their love language is. Dr. Gary Chapman presents that there are five key love languages: appropriate physical touch (like a pat on the back), words of affirmation (Atta boy!), gifts (promotion), acts of service (take over a project), and quality time (company team building events such as bowling or fishing trips).[16] You can usually tell a person's love language by observing what they do for others. If someone is constantly serving a fellow team member or their leadership, attempting to lighten their burden, she's likely going to own acts of service as a love language. If someone is always complimenting everyone around him, he's probably big on words of affirmation. If someone is always inviting a variety of team members to lunch, he may enjoy gifts. And if she's always meeting her co-worker at the gym before their shift starts, she probably enjoys quality time. It's not difficult to figure out the love languages of others when we pay attention to those around us.

People like to know that their leader has witnessed them doing well. Not acknowledging it can leave some team members disgruntled. When we work hard to serve with a spirit of excellence, we like to know our effort has made a difference. When we've helped the company succeed in meeting its goals, we like to be acknowledged for that help. How we're satisfied with that acknowledgement is going to vary from person to person. Some will prefer the raise versus the pat on the back and Atta boy! It's important to get to know our team members well enough to know what will speak to them the greatest. Yes, raises should happen based on performance, evaluations, and results. But it's also important to acknowledge when a team member has grown exponentially between those reviews and offer compensation accordingly.

Another facet of reward is acknowledging the met goal due to the cooperative efforts of the team. We've all heard about the companies who take their teams to the ball game or on the fishing trip or to the

Broadway show. These team building activities promote growth through encouragement. I'd like to suggest there are other activities that may or may not cost as much and would be rewarding for our teams in order to celebrate a success rather than targeting growth. Things that come to mind are to schedule a day off so they can rest and recharge, a day hike in the mountains or a trip to the beach to get away from the hustle and bustle of the day-to-day grind. Whatever the reward may be, the key is to be sure to acknowledge our team's hard work and achievements and applaud them for a job well done.

TAKEOUT:

▶ Don't hold back on encouraging your team members. This is not an area in which to be stingy. Everyone loves encouragement.

▶ Figure out how your team members each receives encouragement best and be sure to use that method to demonstrate your appreciation for them and their hard work.

Build up and empower a winning team
to make your guests feel like #1.
LARRY STUART HOSPITALITY

8

Empowering the Spirit of Hospitality

The best executive is the one who has sense enough to pick good men
to do what he wants done, and self-restraint enough to keep from
meddling with them while they do it.
- THEODORE ROOSEVELT

What we really want to accomplish is to set up a self-sustaining business model that allows for our team members to run the business. Servant leaders depend on those around them and delegate work. We can't be everyone and do everything. No leader has time to do it all. Sometimes it's difficult for leaders to delegate tasks and empower others to do what's required to satisfy a guest. Type A personalities tend to want to cling to control, hyper-managing everything and neglecting to delegate responsibilities. In order to do so, we need to be able to let go and trust that those we've trained know how to do their job well and will do it to their best ability. We must administrate the work so that everyone can succeed.

If we don't delegate the work and empower our staff to do their best work, we open the door for all sorts of issues, including becoming physically and mentally run down, which will eventually result in oversight and mistakes. When we allow our team to do their jobs, we are then able to focus only on what's necessary with great attention to detail. And if our team is empowered to fulfill their responsibilities, business will improve. When we remove that ability, we take out the leaven and are left with dough that never rises—our team members or our business.

Empowering our team members doesn't mean we're going to give them the reigns of the corporation and allow them to run it. Empowerment means giving staff members an entrepreneurial opportunity by providing them with the support, coaching, training, and authority to make one-time, on-the-spot decisions for the benefit of the guest and our establishment. We are losing too many guests who have made the decision to walk out of our operations due to a lack of concern for their challenges. They should not have to stand around and wait while our team members seek out the approval of five different leaders in order to provide guest service recovery. By having the authority to make decisions, our team will have a much easier job of satisfying guests and fellow staff members. The key is for leadership to give others the ability to make decisions and get the work done. If our team members feel like they constantly need to ask permission in order to accomplish their tasks, they'll stagnate and never get anything done. We need to be sure we've empowered them to make wise decisions so they can work instead of standing around waiting for answers from a boss who's too busy to provide them.

The first step to ensuring we're empowering our team members is to be sure a strong work ethic is in place through our company's core values, as well as in our team. We spoke earlier about hiring the best individuals for all positions. Now we're going to look at empowering them to fulfill their responsibilities. One of the things we want to be sure they understand is that we are called to go above and beyond the status quo. Many workers only do what's required to keep their position because they need to provide for themselves or their family. Unfortunately, not everyone loves what they do. You've seen them: the server who provides your drink and never comes back to refill it, the cashier who never offers a sincere smile or says a word, and the airline flight attendant who methodically goes through the routine of safety instructions without an ounce of personality, fun, or passion involved. No one wants to be served by that person.

Have you ever been in a public bathroom and watched as another adult misses the garbage can with their freshly used paper towel? Pride looks at the piece of soiled paper towel on the bathroom floor and says, "It's not my job as the server to clean up the bathroom mess." The team player will take the two seconds to bend over and pick up the trash and put it in the garbage receptacle. As a result, the next guest who walks through that bathroom door won't be disgusted by the condition of the bathroom and decide not to come back the next time she's hungry for Italian food. There are no departmental boundaries when we have an integral team in place. Servers help check in guests. Engineers offer assistance to guests at the pool. The bellman offers assistance in another department. Why? Because they want the guest to know how much they care. This is the spirit of hospitality in action and where servant leaders are born. They do whatever it takes to improve all deliverables, regardless of their place in any particular department. By making certain our team understands our core values, we have empowered them to take ownership of our culture, their position and its responsibilities, and even in the business itself. But most importantly, they've taken ownership of serving our guests with a spirit of hospitality.

The second step to empowering our team members is to be certain their responsibilities are clear and to provide any necessary additional support through training. This ensures our performance expectations are achievable. Answer any questions they may have. A key component to our company's growth, as well as our team members' growth, is that they have confidence in their abilities to do their jobs and do them well. It is equally important that everyone's expectations are qualified up front by asking the right questions and appointing independent mentor coaches to assess the individuals' monthly, quarterly, and annual roles and goals and perform their evaluations. Supervisors, directors, or partners are these mentor coaches. This will insure integrity through the team service delivery process and provide honest results to best drive future productivity, high morale, low turnover, and ROI.

Taking Ownership

What You Expect to Be Tomorrow = How You Deliver Purpose
& Passion Today
– LARRY STUART HOSPITALITY

Once our team members know their job descriptions and how to fulfill them successfully, we need to give them the right to make decisions and make sure they know they have the freedom to do so. If we allow them the ability to do their job without having to stop to ask permission to make key decisions, more can be accomplished in a day—not only for the staff member, but for us servant leaders, as well. The empowered entrepreneur will work beyond their job descriptions and do so with confidence and excellence. We want our team members to operate in their departments as if they owned that department. What would you do differently if your blood, sweat, and tears—as well as dollars—were invested in your employer's company? You'd take ownership. No one will work harder, faster, and smarter than the individual who believes in the company he or she is working for and feels as if they're making a wise investment of their time while on the job. These are crew members who are now part of the bigger picture, not just their job description. By empowering them, we have given them permission to become greater than themselves and grow into the leaders of tomorrow as they carry the spirit of hospitality throughout the service process.

Innovative Input

The success of empowerment depends on the input of the individual team member. Hospitality staff who have taken ownership of their positions—and their place within our company—will begin to recognize a variety of things, including but not limited to issues within our system, inadequacies, others who are working hard and deserve recognition, and guest complaints that are most frequently made. But they won't stop there. They'll provide insight on how to fix it. The people "on the job" know the problems and causes better than anyone. A wise leader will listen when a team member brings something to the table for discussion and resolution.

Innovators break the paradigm of how everyone else thinks. They do the opposite of what the average person would do by stepping out of the box and creating something new, something unique. They see a challenge and solve it, providing solutions to our inconveniences. Innovators set themselves apart from the rest, because they're in the forefront of our competitive society. They are the first to solve the future needs of consumers by exceeding their expectations. These are the people we want on our team, because they'll always be looking to improve the efficiency, presentation, and process of our guest service delivery.

When a team member comes to us with an idea on how to improve production, we need to be careful not to treat them like they're trying to put down our company. Having fresh ideas is innovative, not rebellious. Being a united team involves being of and working as one accord. It means we share the same goal and have the same vision as to how we're going to achieve it while increasing its value. As leaders in hospitality, we need to listen with ears to hear and be open to change, providing that change will continue to take us in the same direction toward excellent guest service rather than derailing the dining car. Both team members and leaders can equally learn from allowing visionaries to use their gifts. Doing so provides essential ingredients for growth while building trust and success in our business relationships.

Hearing from team members makes room for expansion of the parameters of decision making. When we've given the team member an opportunity to express their concerns for a more seamless operation, we leaders gain insight into how they process challenges and design resolutions. Trust evolves. Not only do we begin to trust they can make a solid decision, but they begin to trust that we have both our internal and external guests' best interests at heart. And guess what happens? They take even more ownership of their place in our corporation.

Our goal in allowing for innovative input is to foster a comprehensive vision of continuous improvement. In order to empower our staff members to grow in this aspect, we can allow them the following responsibilities:

1. **Realize and operate from their own power.** Empowerment means team members will begin making relevant, better, and successful choices. They will recognize and value the strength of their own expertise, knowledge, and potential. Recognizing they can make a difference based on what they are capable of doing will boost their personal resolve and morale. Encourage your team members to keep their focus on what they *can* do, rather than what they think they can't do—or what they've always done. Sometimes we may need to change or try something new. It's not always easy, but it's required in order to improve our life, as well as our performance within that life.

2. **Understand their role in the vision of the establishment.** Encourage your team members to create a personal vision for themselves based on your establishment's vision. In doing so, they can determine what gives them energy and provides them with enriched job satisfaction. Once this vision is established, it's important to always keep their vision in the forefront of their mind and how it relates to their success and the success of the establishment. One way to do so is to allow space for a vision board. It doesn't take much to place a bulletin board in the staff lunch room and fill it with images and statements from your team that declare the company's vision. You may even consider putting up a second board where team members can share images and statements that express their personal vision as well. Some may find they have things in common with not only the company, but each other. This bonds team members to grow further with a deeper commitment to each other and our company.

3. **Build their base for action.** When building a base for ourselves, we need to gather the information we need to make wise decisions.

In doing so, we become empowered. What do we need to know to do our job more effectively? What do we need to know to become more competent? This requires getting the "big picture" of our work and how it fits in with the total workings of the hotel, restaurant, or airline. The skill of effective listening is essential for gathering information. This is the responsibility I needed to work on most as I began my career in hospitality. Steven Covey summed it up well for me with his fifth habit in *The 7 Habits of Highly Effective People*, "Seek first to understand and then to be understood."[17]

4. **Take action and let their "magic" shine.** Empowering team members helps them to recognize they have a lot to offer. We need to allow them to look for ways to contribute their knowledge, skills, and ideas most effectively. This involves permitting them to communicate openly. They need to be free to share their ideas, thoughts, feelings, and concerns. This contributes greatly to providing the information others need and is often the key to solving challenges. Clear and consistent communication is essential to effective empowerment.

   Team members must be able to take responsible risks and stretch themselves in order to grow. A necessary part of risk taking is learning to accept failure and view it as an opportunity for growth through the learning experience. When done appropriately and effectively, they are able to take responsible risks, calculate and weigh the possible costs—who and what is affected by their decision—and to discover the consequences of taking that risk, how they are affected. Then they must act on their best calculations, vision, and forecast.

   Another part of their action is owning guest/team member challenges. When a guest explains a problem to a staff member, the one who hears the complaint owns it. We always want to encourage our team to take more responsibility. They need to think of this responsibility as an opportunity to contribute more to their success and the success of the operation. When they know their skills and knowledge, believe in themselves and their abilities, they will become willing to take risks that draw on their strengths. As they do so, they improve their guest service skills and become better at serving the vision of our company.

Allow room for team members to break away from policies in order to better respond to guest needs. Not every guest has the same need, and not every need is addressed adequately in the team member handbook or corporate policies. During the early days of his career, Ron Brennan made an important guest service decision that was far above his paygrade, which financially cost the company. His leader told him what he did was correct, though. He stated, "Always do what is in the best interest of the guest for the company. The standard practice manual is a guide, not the bible." Breaking from policy to satisfy a guest will only be a win-win. Of course, it's best to give our staff some guidelines as to acceptable solutions to challenges. But just as a guest will know the difference between a fresh or frozen fish product, they'll know when the service response is natural versus canned.

Finally, when taking action, our team members must understand that asking for help is not a sign of weakness, but of belief in themselves and their abilities. There's never a stupid question—only smart team members. As management and leaders of the business, we can be a major source of help and support, as can other staff—not only in the person's department, but in other departments as well.

5. **Look for ways to perfect the system.** As we mentioned before, innovators will see a need and work to find a way to fulfill it. We want our staff to become team players. They should always be asking how they can make service smoother, make someone else's job easier, or help the team's effort. Listening to the ideas, needs, and concerns of others creates unity as we become more like-minded. As much as possible, we all need to be flexible and adaptable to these ideas, needs, and concerns of others. We need

to always be aware of opportunities for improvement, both in our own contribution and in the service of the department. Becoming a problem solver is empowering.

Servant Leaders Are Present

Once we've empowered our team members to serve in their fullest capacity, we need to set goals for our individual team members that serve the goals of the team, which then in turn serve the goals of the entire company. Servant leaders will facilitate reaching the goal that has been set. There is a difference between a manager and a leader. A manager is a mechanism that makes the wheel go around. Leaders are the center bore of the wheel itself, supporting the weight of the entire machine. They work alongside their team members with care and concern, empowering their success. The managers of yesterday lack the entrepreneurial compassion of today's leaders.

We must enable and empower those serving so that they may successfully meet the goal we've set. This could look like extra training, mentoring, working the floor alongside our team, making certain guests' needs are being met while our staff does the work, or resolving any issues that arise during execution of the plan. We must be present. Sincere support looks a lot like coming alongside those who you're in authority over. Not only do we serve those who are our boss, we serve those whose boss we are. When we do so with a spirit of hospitality, it becomes empowering to our team members, and they can then serve the guest in the same manner. Be a servant leader who is present. Your team will appreciate it and recognize your commitment to them.

TAKEOUT:

The best thing you can do for your team members is empower them to do their jobs well and provide a system of accountability so they can take responsibility for their mistakes, failures, and successes.

The best leaders hold themselves accountable.
LARRY STUART HOSPITALITY

9

Accountability

A man must be big enough to admit his mistakes, smart enough to
profit from them, and strong enough to correct them.
- JOHN C. MAXWELL

We cannot function in the spirit of hospitality if we refuse to be held accountable for all that we do. Without accountability, people are left to their own will. When we're trying to build a business based on serving others, putting others first is key to our success. Left to our own will—to do what we, personally, see as the best word to say or action to take—our motives become selfish, and we no longer put others before ourselves. We stray from corporate culture and the goal we're trying to achieve together. Accountability allows for us to remember we are here to serve as a team and that in order to do so, we must align ourselves with that corporate vision, values, and culture. We must fulfill our responsibilities as members of a team in order for the entire team to be effective in meeting its goals, which should ultimately be to deliver an excellent, unforgettable experience for our guests.

Team Members Must Be Accountable

Once our team understands how to properly perform their various tasks, they need to follow through on what they've been taught. Accountability will keep the team members on task and keep work flowing seamlessly.

We hold our team members accountable because we want to consistently increase productivity, thereby improving guest service.

There are four general ways in which we may hold our team members accountable.

1. **Review their performance.** This review is generally held quarterly, biannually, or annually. During training, be sure to let the team members know when these reviews are. Most will expect them to occur on time and on target, providing them with vital information, redirection, praise, and a continued opportunity to grow through the process. If we see a team member needs further training, correction, or redirection before their review, we shouldn't wait to provide what is necessary. It's better to do so as needed so their guest service leadership skills can improve in a timely manner.

   When reviewing a team member's performance, refer to past feedback. Let them know if someone has spoken well of their service skills. It's always encouraging to hear you've done a good job. Unlike a raise after an annual review, this form of feedback and recognition creates an inner sense of purpose because the team member has developed a stronger work ethic, served others with professionalism, and operated in the spirit of hospitality. It's a personal success for the team member, so they will internalize the recognition at a more personal level than a monetary compensation ever would.

   Next, describe their current performance. Are they succeeding in an area? Do they need to work on something? Do you have any recommendations?

   Then, describe the desired performance. Remind them of their responsibilities and, if necessary, bring correction or redirection. Set a goal with the team member that they can achieve within a given amount of time before you will conduct another review with them. What we want is to get the team member to commit to the necessary change, which will require action on their part.

Once we've reviewed our team members, we need to follow up with them. Is their performance heading in the right direction, increasing productivity with positive results? Do they need further assistance? It's important to give them an opportunity to let us know if something isn't working so we can fix it before it interferes with our guests' expectations. It's easier to fix the team member's attitude or lack of skill than it is to get a guest to return.

2. **Redirect.** If the team member is struggling in an area or more, we need to be considerate in how we speak to them. Instruction and reprimand are best received when spoken with kindness. We've all heard of the praise sandwich. We start with a kind or encouraging word, suggest how to improve in an area, and conclude with support and encouragement. Redirection will likely result in improvement by the next review. It may be a good idea to provide more training if necessary. You may also wish to consider providing feedback every week if it will help provide accountability as your team members are learning new skills, correcting areas of struggle, or practicing innovation. Coming alongside our team is always encouraged.

3. **Reward.** If your team member is performing as expected over a long period of time, consider rewarding them with a raise or bonus at the end of the year. If they're performing as expected plus innovating solutions to issues, consider a potential change in position—up the ranks. These must be standardized in your company's team member handbook so that when you reward performance, it is consistently done and maintains equality in the workplace.

4. **Removal.** As much as we hate to do it, sometimes we just need to let someone go. If we've reviewed, redirected, trained further, and the team member hasn't acceptably responded, he's already made his choice and quit, whether he's let leadership know or not. Maybe he never fully committed to being part of the vision to begin with. Matters of this kind are prominent throughout the workforce,

not because leadership hasn't provided the optimum hospitality opportunity, but because some people just aren't interested in moving forward with us and have chosen not to do so. At this point, we need to let him know it isn't working out. We don't want to keep someone in a position they don't enjoy or may not want to be in. This won't do anything except deter company morale and cause issues with the team and their functionality. As they say, the weak link breaks the chain and needs to be remedied as soon as possible. Never be afraid to fire someone who doesn't want to be a part of our team or do their job. Replace him with someone who would appreciate the opportunity and be a much better fit.

There's one more review we need to talk about. It's the company review. At least once a year, we should meet with our team members to find out how they see the company and its leadership—us—are doing. What do they see that needs to change? What do they see that isn't working? Are there any issues with leadership? It's important to listen to our staff, because they are the front line who are serving our guests. They hear and see more complaints and accolades than leadership ever will, which gives them an inside view.

Accountable Leaders

Bob Reppin remembers driving from Orlando, Florida after opening the Hyatt Grand Cypress—the company's first luxury resort—to Hilton Head, South Carolina to renovate the Hyatt House and reposition it as a Hyatt Regency. He had viewed Hyatt food and beverage directors as "gods" and had never thought he would reach that level. This would be his debut as a director, and it dawned on him that now he would be expected to be a "god" too. While he was driving, it hit him hard that he was no god and was now responsible for his staff's careers, his guests' experiences, and the owner's financial return. It was one of many pivotal moments in his life. For the rest of his trip, he examined the things that got him where he was, and he realized he had to maintain the course he was on, now more than ever. Bob knew he was responsible and would be held accountable for his genuine sincerity and approachability with his team, his commitment to excellence no matter what it took, and the opportunity to create true partnerships with every person at every level of the business.

Our team members aren't the only ones who need to be held accountable. Leaders must understand they are responsible for and accountable to those who depend on them. Being accountable to our team members may seem daunting. Aren't they accountable to us? Don't we make sure they are accomplishing their tasks, earning their paychecks? Yes, but this is where being in a position of authority is humbling. The leader who can be accountable to his or her team members is the leader who will be recognized as putting others before themselves. When we are responsible to our staff and allow them to let us know when we've let them down or have not enabled them to serve our guest in an appropriate manner, we can make a difference in their success by allowing them to call us on it. It shows that we don't see ourselves as any better than they are. We're all human. *We all fall short of the mark.* We can fail together. And, we can celebrate our wins together.

As leaders, it's our responsibility to set the pace and walk the talk. Especially when it comes to errors. Too often, leadership focuses on the wrongdoing of their team members, when the real issue is their personal neglect of that team. Part of being a servant leader is knowing that when a situation goes wrong, we have a responsibility and the ability to make it right. We must show a sincere interest and take the initiative to do so.

If you aren't part of one, you probably know someone who is a member of a dysfunctional family. The problem with dysfunctional families is that treating one another with love, kindness, and respect has gotten lost somewhere in the family tree. Someone forgot the golden rule to treat one another the way they want to be treated. Of course, some people don't love themselves, which makes it difficult to love others. What we need to recognize is that as leaders, we should always treat our staff with compassion, kindness, respect, courtesy, and consideration. We must be able to identify our flaws and allow for change. No one is perfect, and we'll all make mistakes at one point or another. Servant leaders will always take the high road. We do the right thing for the right reason, no matter the expense. We recognize we've got others following us, and we set the right example by maintaining integrity in the work place.

Early in my career, I learned from fellow leader Bill Rizzuto that there is a time and place for discipline and praise. We don't want to consistently praise a team member in front of others, because it becomes patronizing. At the same time, we don't want to tear into someone or even discipline them in front of others. That's just plain embarrassing—and not only for the staff member. Others are watching us leaders at all times, whether we acknowledge that or not. Tearing into a fellow teammate reveals a heart that isn't operating in the spirit of hospitality, and the staff who are listening to that discourse will see our hypocrisy, which tears down trust in an instant. If the team member has made a mistake, we need to gently call it to their attention—behind closed doors, not in front of their fellow teammates.

Challenges should be issued gently, honestly, and directly with sincerity, calling team members higher. No one likes or appreciates being corrected by being shamed, blamed, or in a verbally or emotionally abusive manner. We want to address the issue, not the person's character. Character development will follow if you avoid bullying tactics to try to gain compliance.

If we make a mistake, we need to own that. Servant leaders take responsibility for their actions. If a team member fails because we didn't properly prepare them to handle a situation with a guest, we need to own that we dropped the plate. We cannot be blame shifting or degrading our team members.

Correction is best received from a gentle tongue, behind closed doors, and learning happens best when the teaching is done with kindness. Treat them like family—good family, not dysfunctional family. Then the staff will follow leadership and treat the guests with the same respect, courtesy, and kindness. And that's a win for everyone.

Accountability to Guests

In every business, things will go wrong. We have to admit that—no matter how much we hate to—because they do and they will. When things go wrong that are beyond our guests' control, whether on our end or theirs, we need to not only have empathy but to do everything in our power to correct the error. Yes, errors cost, but we can certainly minimize the damage if we are proactive about resolution. Don and Andi were flying Alaska Airlines when taking a trip to Seattle. Due to a mechanical issue, they were delayed a few hours at LAX. Alaska Airlines issued all of their passengers on the delayed flight a $100 voucher to be used on any flight to make up for their inconvenience. The vouchers were in their inboxes before they got off the flight in Seattle. Those vouchers told their passengers that Alaska Airlines cares about their clients and values their time.

I mentioned that this accountability to our guests also needs to be in place when the situation is beyond not only the guest's control but ours as well. Andi and Don had scheduled a trip to Cabo San Lucas when Don discovered via a website that it wasn't safe to travel to Mexico due to gang-related violence. Alaska Airlines' guest service specialist was totally empathetic and took five minutes to discuss the situation with a supervisor while Andi was on the phone. The full refund for their trip was immediate, no questions asked. Once again, she received the message that Alaska Airlines truly cares about their passengers.

This kind of accountability will keep guests coming back for more, choosing to spend their funds at our establishments. It's only when we're willing to admit we've made a mistake, our equipment has malfunctioned, or that our guests' priorities and concerns are our priorities and concerns that we can truly say we've been accountable to our guests and upheld the vision and cultural standards we've set for our businesses.

TAKEOUT:

There are three areas where we need accountability in business:

1. Leadership
2. Team members
3. Guest service

As servant leaders, we must be willing to admit our mistakes. Doing so builds trust with both our internal and external guests. Trust leads to loyalty, and loyalty leads to an increase in our bottom line.

Listen more. Talk less.
Always keep others first.
LARRY STUART HOSPITALITY

10

What the Spirit of Hospitality Looks Like to Guests

The guest's perception is your reality.

- KATE ZABRISKIE

Our guest is the most important person in our restaurant or hotel, or on our airline or cruise ship, whether they walk through the front door, call on the phone, or find us online. And each guest is going to have a different experience based on their unique, individual personalities, past experiences, and current expectations or desires. They are just like us, with feelings and emotions, biases and prejudices. The wise businessman or businesswoman is going to cater to the individual guest, not give a one-size-fits-all performance hoping to please everyone and keep the workload simple. Instead, we're going to work to understand what the guest is looking for and provide a solution that will exceed the desire of every guest who walks through the door, meeting their needs individually so they have a unique experience and will want to return for another. Our overall attitude should reflect a positive spirit of genuine hospitality, and this attitude needs to be conveyed to our guests at all times.

We don't invite customers to our house for Thanksgiving dinner. We invite our friends and family—our guests. The same should be true for our business establishments. When we look at people as mere customers, we see volume, dollar signs, and return on our investment. No one likes to be treated like a number. One person who answered my brief guest service survey said, "Nothing bothers me more than when the server brings me my check and I haven't even been asked if I wanted dessert or coffee. Am I taking up space? Do they want to get rid of me to move the next guest in so they can make their subsequent tips? Even when the server says, 'No rush,' I'm now rushing to leave if they haven't offered dessert or coffee/tea." Note that this guest felt as though he or she was a number—tips, taking up space, and hasn't been offered dessert or coffee or tea. No one should be made to feel rushed through their dining experience or like they're only good for tips and turnover. As guest service specialists, we must anticipate when a meal is almost finished and offer coffee and dessert before we ever offer the check.

The most expensive thing in a restaurant is an empty seat. You might say the guest is a good person, but do you know who else she is? She's the person who never comes back and never tells her friends about our establishment. It amuses her to see us spend money every year to try to get her back to our business when she was there in the first place and all we had to do to keep her business was show her a little courtesy.

Another guest shared a story of being on a flight when an attendant asked her to move to the back of the plane "to help balance it." Another passenger was immediately shown to her purchased seat. If this doesn't upset you, it should. Since when do we treat our guests as if they were second best? When we honor those who patronize our establishments in the same manner we would treat a guest breaking bread with us in our personal homes, we see people who matter. Without our guests, we have no business, which means we need to treat them with the spirit of hospitality, respect, and appreciation—from the family of eight joining us for their vacation stay to the business mogul or celebrity who needs a place to stay while they're in town. Each one needs to feel as if they are the celebrity guest. If a guest doesn't feel welcome—like they're in their home away from home—they're not likely to return.

A guest is not an interruption of our work. These individuals are the sole purpose of our work. Rolling our eyes or ignoring a guest are inappropriate responses when we're on the floor. One guest was with a rather large party at a local pizza and brewery when their server became busy with one member of their party and had to find a requested T-shirt, which the restaurant sold. Meanwhile, the rest of the table had already finished their first round of drinks. This guest attempted multiple times to get the attention of the other wait staff, who continually walked past their table without bothering to stop as she held out her empty glass. When she discovered they were all standing nearby at the bar, chatting away, she had to yell out to get their attention and request refills for the entire table. Having worked as a server herself, it irritated her that no one else seemed to notice or care that there was a need and that the table's server wasn't present. It not only reflected poorly on the rest of the wait staff, it reflected poorly on the leadership, who are accountable for such service failures. A servant leader would have taken note that the table's service sequence wasn't synchronized or being properly managed. Our guests don't want our service staff hovering over them, but they do want occasional eye contact in case something is required. Consistent, invisible service is the best service.

It makes people smile when their server is in the moment and focusing 150 percent on serving them from the heart—not looking over his shoulder and busy like the rest of us. Another guest said, "It makes me nervous when people take my order without writing it down. Are they going to remember a table full of peoples' orders by the time they reach the kitchen or computer system? Even if it's just my husband and me, it makes me nervous. There's too much opportunity to forget something or get something wrong." Imagine how that guest will feel if he's busy looking away while taking that order. Our guests want to know we are focused on serving them and hopefully exceeding their needs. Anything less will leave them wanting more.

Several guests who completed my survey also mentioned they desire a quality experience without breaking the bank. Our guests shouldn't have to pay for better service. It should be the calling card of our business, regardless of price. They expect great service value throughout their experience, whether their check is for $27.50 or $127.50, and we should genuinely deliver it. When we strive to save money and skimp on service, it hurts our business' bottom line. I'll choose better service over product every time, and our guests will too. People want to be served sincerely, professionally, and with heartfelt care.

Larger families are also concerned about cost. They don't always have the funds to afford multiple hotel rooms or airline tickets when attempting to take a family vacation. Most hotels only accommodate four to a room and promote adjoining rooms for larger families. One guest wonders if leadership has considered that means separating a husband and wife into two rooms, splitting the family that would really prefer to stay together. Most suites don't even accommodate a family larger than five or six, and suites tend to be more expensive than staying in two adjoining rooms. Add teens into the mix, and families are now paying adult prices, jacking up the price per room. Our guests would like us to know they want us to listen to their concerns and requirements. This would include stopping the price jacking and saying things like, "You get what you pay for." They're tired of our upselling and pushing sales, as well as being taken advantage of in order to travel with their family. Kids are still kids until they turn eighteen. Yes, they may eat a little more, but not always. And they don't take up extra space in a normal bed. What we need to keep in mind is that we are building our brand relations into the next generation, who will patronize our establishments if we market well and go about that guest-establishment relationship properly.

More Service Turnoffs

As if the above guest concerns weren't enough, there are ten service turnoffs I've seen to be abundant during my years in guest services. These are:

1. **The soup of the day is, "I'll find out."** Our service staff should know the menu front to back and back to front. There's no excuse for not knowing the specials, menu details, wines, and so on.

2. **Auctioning food**, as in, "Now, who gets the BLT, burger, or steak?" We need to be training our staff to start taking orders at one side of the table and going clockwise so they can note by position who gets what food and drinks. If we have someone else serving the food, they too should know the order sequence.

3. **Messy restrooms.** There's no excuse for a messy environment anywhere in our facility. This is another of our guests' concerns. They want to come into a warm, inviting, and *consistently sanitary* environment.

4. **Seating guests at a table with a tip on it.** Guests should always be seated at a clean, orderly, set table.

5. **Greeting the guest with a single word, such as, "Two?"** Always greet our guests with an inviting, warm, and professional welcome. Remember, they're not a number. They're people just like us with emotions, needs, and desires. And they're guests, not customers.

6. **Having dirty plates in hand when talking to a guest.** This is never a good practice. Granted, they will occasionally stop us to ask for condiments or a refill on their drinks, but we should never intentionally stop to talk to guests while we're clearing a table.

7. **Not knowing who's drinking what.** "Uh, was that a Diet Coke?"

8. **"Discussion groups" of servers hanging around in the back of the room**—or by the bar while the server is downstairs finding a T-shirt for a guest at the table where everyone else is waiting for refills on their drinks because the food isn't ready yet.

9. **Not acknowledging waiting guests.** All it takes is a small acknowledgement. "It shouldn't be much longer. May I offer you a glass of water while you're waiting? Please know how much we appreciate your patience." This lets our guests know we've seen them and know that they are important to us. It also demonstrates that we value their time. They may be headed to a movie or concert

after dinner, so it's important to keep that in mind. Always keep them informed. Communication demonstrates how much we care.

10. **Pouring coffee from stained pots into cold cups.** These are cleanliness and serving issues. No one wants their food or drink served at the wrong temperature or on anything that appears to not have been properly cleaned. Silverware also needs to be checked and polished before it is rolled and presented. Guests don't want to eat off something that has food crusted on it or is spotted from going through the dishwasher.

The spirit of hospitality takes a person from being a customer and elevates them to being a guest. We should always operate in it.

Please Hear Me

Another common customer complaint is that the guest service provider has not responded in a way that says they heard the guest's concern. We're all familiar with the one guest who calls so many times that the front desk attendant no longer answers their calls. Tonia's guest was hung up on a billing issue, and no matter how many times her front desk staff explained it in the past, the guest just didn't seem to get it.

Ignoring the calls wasn't going to make the issue go away. Tonia decided to take action. She took the time to return the guest's call and invite her in to the office. Tonia was kind in her invitation and offered to take the time to rectify the situation. This made sure her guest didn't feel as if she was getting called to the principal's office. During their visit, Tonia showed the guest exactly what had happened with the billing and why the charge remained on her credit card. Once she had revealed the truth to the guest, she was satisfied with the outcome and the phone calls stopped.

Did it take some time out of Tonia's day to rectify the situation? Yes. Was it convenient? No. But it did accomplish what it needed to, and the front desk associates no longer had to deal with multiple phone calls per week from a guest who didn't understand their bill.

Guests want to know that we care enough to listen to their concerns and solve their problems efficiently and amicably. They want to know we hear them and they deserve our immediate response. If our team members aren't sure how to respond, then it's our job as leadership to honor our guest with a phone call or invitation to visit our office.

It's All About the Guest

Guest service is not about how wonderful we are. It's not about what we can or have achieved. It's about serving our guests with excellence. It's about having the attitude that even the simplest of jobs is as important as being the CEO of the company. In the hospitality business, we need to have the ability to anticipate the guests' needs. When we're in front of the guests' every move, we can surprise them at every turn throughout their experience. This will exceed their expectations and provide a memorable experience. There are a few things we can do that will allow this to occur:

1. **Eye contact:** Recognize the guest first, before they get to you, and acknowledge her presence through eye contact. This demonstrates we care for them, that we're on our game, and that we are there to serve their every need.
2. **Sincere smile:** This gift must be presented with eye contact. Guests will know if our greeting is sincere and from our heart.
3. **The appropriate hospitality comment:** The appropriate hospitality comment should be yours to start and finish when serving. For example, "Thank you for joining us today, Mr. Mandel. We appreciate that you've chosen our facility and look forward to exceeding your expectations. We hope to have you back to join us soon."

Whether you served a particular guest or not, be sure to thank them for visiting your establishment. Tell them you look forward to seeing them again soon. Remember, the guest belongs to everyone. It's our responsibility to protect that. This concept is imperative to sustain and viably grow our business relationships.

TAKEOUT:

Overall, the key things our guests want are:

▸ to be noticed
▸ to be treated like they matter
▸ to be served—and perceive that the server cannot wait for the opportunity and pleasure of serving them
▸ to be welcomed into a warm, inviting environment

If we can master these requirements of the spirit of hospitality, we'll be providing excellent guest service and find our business growing as our guests come back—with their friends.

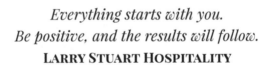

Everything starts with you.
Be positive, and the results will follow.
LARRY STUART HOSPITALITY

11

Generosity

Giving is the highest level of living.
- JOHN C. MAXWELL

People with a generous spirit are always ready to give of themselves and their time and their resources, expecting nothing in return for their gift. Instead, they thrive on the joy of blessing others. Reward is a sense of purpose. We can't buy this with silver or gold. We can only find it within.

Every time my father had gigs singing at the Persian Room at the Park Plaza in New York City, he'd put a box of clothes in the back of his Ferrari. Then he'd park at Columbus Circle in Manhattan and give the attendant the box of clothes. He'd also leave generous tips for the bellmen, Maître D, stage crew, and others—on top of the gift of the clothing. Why was Dad so gracious with tips? Because he came from nothing and wanted to pass on the generosity value to people less fortunate. He paid it forward.

Although he provided me with an incredible life, a Cornell University degree, and the wisdom I live by and cherish today, Dad never gave me anything for free. He understood the value of hard work and wanted me to succeed in learning the same value. But when he saw a need, he did what he could to meet it. In 1975, I was working 12- to 15-hour kitchen shifts at the Alameda Plaza in Kansas City, Missouri. One day, Dad called to say he was coming to town and wanted to visit with me. I was at work, so he asked if he could stop by my apartment to freshen up. That apartment had a mattress on the floor—no other furnishings. That evening, I came home to fully furnished apartment. He operated in the spirit of hospitality and always told me to go first class or stay home until you can. He said to never go halfway, but first class all the way.

Why do so many people struggle with being generous? Ted Dekker says that "Giving threatens what the flesh thinks must be protected."[18] We don't want to let go of our finances, our knowledge, or other assets because we're afraid someone will take advantage of our generosity and abuse us. We want to protect ourselves from that and cling to what we have. Or, we fear that if we give something away, we'll need it next month. So, we hang onto it instead of blessing another. What we need to realize is that when we give to someone else, we actually end up giving to ourselves. We give ourselves the joy of knowing we've blessed another human being. We get the gift of someone else's smile.

In the hospitality business, we have to allow ourselves to be generous so our guests will be blessed and then we, in turn, will also be blessed. We can't be stingy and hold back. If we do, we shouldn't expect any ROI, because you can't earn a return on something you didn't invest in in the first place. The successes of many businesses are based on the quality of their relationships. Without relationship, we have nothing.

Some days, it's difficult to serve others in a spirit of hospitality. When we understand the spirit of hospitality and can function within its values and principles, we have the ability to think and perform outside of the box, even on those challenging days. This is a new way to operate. It will take our relationships to a new level, bring success and growth at work or in our career paths, our self-worth will increase, our salary will grow, and we will find that peace, purpose, and contentment we've been searching for. Ultimately, operating in a spirit of hospitality will provide the ability to build our career paths through our exceptional guest service delivery.

We're called to give with a joyful heart. Why is that so important? Because our gift is supposed to bless the recipient, and our reward is the joy of knowing we've blessed someone through our service. It's an act of compassion to give something, whether that something is our time, money, or even a simple thing such as a smile. The greatest act of compassion is to lay down one's life for our friend. It's a selfless act—one that guest service specialists should perform every day we go to work. When we recognize that it's better to give than to receive, we realize that giving a gift isn't about expecting to get something back. It's about blessing someone else. Because giving isn't about me. And if it is, then it's not a gift. If we're expecting a return on our gift, then we're loaning something rather than giving it away. Where's the reward in that? There isn't one.

The Greatest Joy Is Giving

When we give of ourselves to others, it brings joy to our heart, a sense of purpose, and helps us feel complete as a person. A life of service is all about blessing others by helping them through something we have already experienced. In hospitality, the joy comes from providing the very best experience to those we have the pleasure of interacting with, whether they be guest, co-worker, or leadership.

When giving a gift, it's important to recognize what our team members appreciate as individuals. Does she prefer an act of service? Words of encouragement? Spending quality time with others? Acceptable physical touch? Or does she prefer receiving tangible gifts? For example, let's say we have a team member who strives to please others. This person is likely to enjoy receiving words of encouragement, and we may find that simply recognizing the job she's done well will perk her up and increase her performance levels. If we have another team member who likes advancement, he may prefer tangible gifts, such as incentives and raises. Knowing how our team members respond to various forms of gifts—such as what we say, incentives, spending time doing a team building activity together, a pat on the back, or when we take the time to organize their cluttered desk (so long as they aren't naturally the type of person who knows where everything is in that clutter)—can help us discover ways to improve our relationship with them and develop a level of trust that will engage them in the workplace.

This translates to the guest services side of the business as well. Maybe a guest would receive a word of kindness better than a freebie. Maybe moving a worn-out mother and her toddler up to that empty first-class seat would change her day for the positive. Look for ways to ease someone else's perceived pain. They won't forget it and will remember the service they received for a long time. We may win a lifelong guest who will tell all her friends about how great flying with our airline was. Which will only lead to growth in business. Giving a gift doesn't have to be a grand thing, either. Gifts can be simple, thoughtful, and meaningful. It doesn't take a lot to bless another person. Consider what they enjoy, and work from there.

Barb and her daughter visited the local Chuy's when she was visiting for a few weeks. During the course of their dinner, Barb mentioned to their server that Chuy's was always at the top of her list of places she'd like to go while in town. As they finished dining, the manager approached their table carrying a beautifully presented plate of Tres Leches Cake.

"I heard you love coming here, and we just wanted to say thank you for visiting us during your stay." He set the plate on the table. "This is on us."

Barb and her daughter were blown away by his generosity.

What did it take for them to be blessed? An attentive server and a responsive leader. Did it cost a fortune to do something generous? No. It was a piece of cake.

Beware of Greed

The opposite of a giving spirit is greed. Beware of this green monster that only has eyes for what he or she can get out of any relationship or situation. Greed is only out for herself. She loves to take and struggles with giving. If we've got a team member who only seems to be out for themselves and what they can obtain, it may be time to release them into the world to find another job. Greedy people will suck the life out of the work environment. They'll step over others to reach a higher status in the company. They'll treat guests with disdain, leaving them feeling as if they weren't sincerely cared for. These are not the kind of people we want on our hospitality teams.

Going the Extra Mile

What difference did the Good Samaritan make? He went the extra mile. He made promises and he kept them. He was an honorable man with a good heart toward others, no matter the cost and despite who society said they were and how they should be treated. Every guest and every team member desires to know they are important. Servant leaders need to be willing to go the extra mile for them. We always remember who treated us with kindness and helped us when we needed it—and even when we didn't need it.

Going the extra mile involves providing our guests—both internal and external—the wow factor. Thinking outside of the box, we need creative solutions to issues and impressive incentives. We need to be extraordinary in our service instead of plain ordinary.

Whether you are big or small, you cannot give good guest service if your team members don't feel good about coming to work.
- MARTIN OLIVER

Let's begin with our internal guests—our team members. How do we provide that wow factor for them? Morale is a state of mind based on the attitudes and satisfaction with the organization. When a positive and supportive atmosphere truly exists, high morale is evident. One of the things we want to do is prevent turnover. Keeping morale high amongst our current team members is key to avoiding that turnover. Providing our team members with rewards, incentives, and other generous benefits will keep morale high and turnover low.

Rewards

What do our team members reap if they sow stellar integral performance and achievement? Somewhere in our training structure should be rewards.

They should be standardized and consistent. We need to provide a report card for our team members' performances in quantified blocks of time. This can be done monthly, quarterly, biannually, or yearly. By measuring their results and setting incentive goals, their yearly statistics will propel them to sow so they can then reap the benefit of their reward. This all comes down to their ability and passion to excel personally and as a member of the team.

The key to giving reward is to find out how our team members receive encouragement. We discussed this a bit earlier in this chapter. If we can figure out how our team members enjoy receiving encouragement for their achievements, we'll have a good idea how to reward them. Now, let's take a deeper look in the context of rewarding our internal guests.

Words of affirmation would look like encouragement. "Job well done!" Remember the stickers we received at the top of our elementary grade papers? Smiley faces and gold stars? Those are words of affirmation to a six-year-old. What incentives could you give an adult team member? Do you offer a cruise or trip to Walt Disney World or a culinary trip to Tuscany to the top earners in your business each year? That would speak wonders to someone who values quality time. Bonuses work well for team members who enjoy prizes, as do above-the-average raises. If someone is encouraged by physical touch, a pat on the back or grasp of the shoulder or shake of the hand work well. I shouldn't have to clarify this, but for the sake of being sure it's known, I will. Physical touch should never be sexual—or mistakably sexual, for that matter—in the work place. It's uncalled for and uninvited, so be sure your touch is not overly personal but instead respectable, professional, and understood to be received that way. What about those who like acts of service? An act-of-service reward could be allowing a team member to take an extra day off, relieving a menial task from their schedule for a period of time, or moving them into a bigger station or office. Get to know your staff and what types of rewards speak to them. Don't be afraid to ask, either. Well-rewarded team members take ownership of their responsibilities and the company's vision. Having their buy-in is critical for everyone's expectations to be achieved. Promote your company by promoting your team members.

Incentives

One area most companies have realized they cannot skimp on is incentives. Team members have come to realize their need for a healthy lifestyle. This means we are more focused on physical fitness, healthy eating options, family, and rest. We have begun to understand that we can't keep going and going and expect to perform at our peak when we've run ourselves into the ground. Company incentives are one area we can afford to be generous in today's competitive market.

1. **Incentive-based Compensation:** This type of compensation allows for the team member to strive to increase their personal return on investment. Within this structure, there are different levels of compensation. A team member may get an incentive per their hourly wage. Then there are bonuses based on how well the operation performs, our gross, bottom-line, or net profit.

2. **Tips:** As a restaurant server, someone may get a percentage of tips for running the food to a guest's table when there isn't a server on the floor. If he or she performs well, hustles, and keeps their servers' guests happy, the food runner may get more from the wait staff at the end of the night.

3. **Designer Benefit Packages:** Allow team members to choose which benefits they want.

4. **Lifestyle Benefits:** These are much more available today, such as on-site daycare, gym memberships, on-site spas, meal perks, and team member discounts. These types of compensation are popular with team members who desire to lead a balanced life—particularly the millennial generation.

However, no compensation beats personal growth. Why is this the best incentive? Because it brings a sense of pride and achievement when we grow and excel in what we do with our gifts and talents. And nothing beats knowing we've overcome a challenge and achieved personal success.

Promotion

Where many would look for qualified leadership externally, the wise CEO would promote from within. Our team members are closer to our business culture, because they've worked and lived it every day they've been on the job with us. It's easier to move someone up from within the company than to try to find someone new who values what we value and has the necessary skills to fill the position.

Promoting from within also encourages our team members to be achievers. People will seek jobs elsewhere if there's no room for advancement at our company. When we notify our team members that there is room for advancement, some will take advantage of that and strive to move up the corporate ladder.

A paycheck can't pay you for your values. When our personal values line up with those of our place of employment, we get far more satisfaction out of a job well done than any dollar amount could ever provide. What we really want is for our team members to love working for us and be so passionate about their work that they won't want to retire until they die. When someone loves their job to that extent, they own it. They find their unique purpose and realize their gifts and talents. However, that also leaves room for them to advance to a better place in life, which could move them beyond our doors. The success for us in that situation would be in knowing we've helped them get there

TAKEOUT:

Giving must come from a heart of service. When it does, there is more joy in that than there ever could be in earning a paycheck.

Some serve customers. We serve guests.
That's why they keep coming back!
LARRY STUART HOSPITALITY

12

Serving the Spirit of Hospitality

Service, in short, is not what you do, but who you are. It is a way of living that you need to bring to everything you do, if you are to bring it to your guest interactions.

- BETSY SANDERS

Hospitality could be defined as inviting guests, who could be strangers, into our home or business so we can provide something to meet their basic needs, such as food, drink, or housing. Typically, we think of paying for such a service—staying at a hotel, dining at a restaurant, getting a drink at the bar. But have we considered that service should be provided for free? Whether someone buys a room, meal, or drink or not? If we want our guests to return, our service should be free of charge and offered with a genuine smile in the spirit of hospitality.

You and I were given the opportunity to be a part of this incredible world in which we live. At this particular time. In this particular place. We only have one shot to give it our all, contribute to a cause, and give back to those around us. To give is the reason we live. Serving others is something we choose to do, whether or not they return the favor. It's the gift we operate in. It's who we are. From the day we are born, we are involved in relationships. With our parents. With our family. With our friends, classmates, coworkers, bosses, spouses, children. Relationships are a never-ending part of life, and we can either learn to live well with others or we can choose to live in strife. Relationships are by no means easy. They require work and dedication.

So does a life of service.

As soon as we're old enough, our parents begin to assign household chores. Clean up your room. Put your dirty dishes in the sink. Take out the trash. We begin to learn that our family is a team, and we are a part of something bigger than ourselves. Our focus begins to turn outward, rather than solely inward. There are people around us who depend on us to do our part in this world. Thus, we begin our life of service to others.

Even though we have different opinions, philosophies, and ideas as to why we are here, we all find ourselves in some type of service role. If you work as a stay-at-home mom, you serve your family. If you work as a teacher, you're serving the students you're teaching. If you work in construction, you're serving the person whose home or warehouse you're building. If you work at Starbucks, you're serving the guests who come in for that coffee and lifestyle experience. Life. Is. Service.

The most satisfying work is helping others. No matter what career we've chosen, there is always an opportunity to help others. We can support a new team member while they are trying to achieve a new skill or learning how to work well with a new leader. We can mentor coworkers who are climbing the ranks by sharing our knowledge, building their confidence, and complimenting their positive results. I always feel most valuable when I've helped someone else. This focused effort brings a much greater reward than money ever will. It acknowledges your place in the world and provides a hope for your future and someone else's future. This is a selfless act—putting our fellow man first. Help one another by being compassionate, useful, and caring.

The key to living a life of service well is compassion. It's compassion for others that gives us the desire to serve them. If we don't care for those we serve, then our service will represent an obligation rather than a joy. Note, the one being served will always be able to tell the difference. It's compassion for others that urges us to go the extra mile, think outside of the box, or go above and beyond. What we have to be careful of is only doing so for those we consider friends. Because that's easy. What's difficult is choosing to walk in a spirit of hospitality toward those we may not enjoy being around—those we may even consider to be our enemy. In the service industry, these people may be grumpy guests. Or the boss who doesn't seem to notice or care about his team members and their personal or work-related challenges. Or the co-worker who would stab you in the back the minute you walk away from the water cooler. We must always choose compassion, taking the high road in every situation.

What does a heart of service look like? Let's take a look at a story most of us know well. It's the tale of a Good Samaritan, a man who served someone despite what others might think of him. A man was traveling from Jerusalem to Jericho when he was robbed, beaten, and stripped naked. The criminals left him half dead. A priest passed by, refusing to help him. Later, a Levite did the same. It was the Samaritan who finally stopped and had compassion on the man. He took care of his wounds, set him on his animal, took him to the inn, and told the innkeeper to see that his needs were met. When he departed the inn the next day, the Samaritan gave the innkeeper two denarii and told him he'd be back to pay whatever the difference was for the beaten man's care. He'd shown mercy on a man everyone else passed by. The Good Samaritan displayed the following five characteristics of someone who truly operates with a servant's heart:

1. **A servant doesn't see labels.** They see an individual in need of assistance. Unfortunately, we live in a world where lines still exist. Lines between black and white. Lines between rich and poor. Lines between north and south, east and west. Those who operate in the spirit of hospitality recognize that these lines shouldn't exist and that compassion needs to precede our differences.

2. **A servant doesn't fear consequences for doing what they see as right.** They focus on meeting a need before more harm is done. Company policy sometimes needs to come second to assistance. Think about the flight attendant who insisted on taking the mother's stroller while she struggled to board the plane with her

children. Company policy said no strollers on board. But couldn't the flight attendant have escorted the mother and her children to their seats, given her a moment to retrieve their items from the stroller, and then offered to check the stroller for her? Where was the attendant typically stationed outside the plane door, assisting passengers with checking their strollers? Sometimes we need to meet the needs of our guests before we meet company policy, because every situation calls for a customized solution. We must allow our team members to operate in the spirit of hospitality, handling every situation accordingly but as they see best fit.

3. **A servant isn't too busy to meet a need.** They take the time to assist another before completing their own task or meeting their own desire. Servants aren't so self-focused they don't notice the need of a guest. Ron Bellomo noted that as hospitality specialists, we must have peripheral vision. There are always ten things going on. Sometimes, we want to give one customer our full attention, but there's something over there that needs five seconds of interaction to resolve it. It's important to know how to continue to give a customer our full attention and deal with the five-second need at the same time.

4. **A servant doesn't bat an eye at what it will cost them to care for another.** They are givers by nature. The story in point number three is a great example of this as well. If a server is walking past tables they aren't waiting on with a full pot of coffee or a fresh pitcher of water, it only takes a moment to stop and fill the cups along the way to their own guests. Will tips really suffer if we take the time to refill drinks at a table that isn't ours? I doubt it.

5. **A servant expects nothing in return.** It's their honor to put others before themselves. They recognize the blessing in giving. Angelo Cipollone was working at the Loews New York Hotel when his director of food and beverage came to him with sincere urgency. "Angelo, I agreed to serve 500 people that are stranded in New York for the evening. The storm is forcing a cruise ship to stay

docked until tomorrow. We have the rooms, but we have to feed them in the restaurant. Can your banquet team help?"

Knowing he was breaking down a big show with tons of staging in the ballroom, he told him to check in the guests and give him a few hours. One has to love the connections available in New York City. He called a friend who set him up with twenty sailor tee shirts, along with a white ship captain jacket and hat. His amazing chef, John, put together pasta stations, carving stations, cheese, fruit, and antipasto displays, and dessert and coffee stations on the fly. Meanwhile, his setup team worked with him to move the existing stages around the ballroom and form a two-level boat with steps, tables, and cocktail tables.

His guests may have been dry docked for the storm, but the ship was sailing in the Embassy Ballroom that night. Dinner was a blast, and the guests couldn't believe how well everything came together. It all worked out well for everyone. Sometimes when we honor others, expecting nothing in return, we set an example someone else can follow. Never say never. There's always an alternative solution.

Genuine Human Interaction

I was managing the grand opening of the Walt Disney World Dolphin and observing how well our team members were performing, when a five-year-old girl took off at a quick pace through the lobby and tripped and fell down on the tile floor. In the process, she dropped her ice cream, cut her knee, and skinned her forehead. I was nearby and immediately ran over to help calm the child and reassure her parents my staff and I were ready to serve. At the same time, I had asked one of my colleagues to notify security to bring a first-aid kit and houseman to clean the floor. Security was immediately on the scene and provided assistance to clean her wounds, offering to place Disney character Band-Aids on both her knee and forehead. The young lady chose Mickey and Minnie to protect her cuts. This served well in calming her down.

Now it was my turn to bring them back to their Disney experience. I asked her parents if I could take their daughter to one of my favorite places in the hotel—the Dolphin Fountain ice cream shop. When we arrived, the crew was performing a 1950s-style coordinated dance, which the little girl loved. I brought her over to the counter and said, "Mickey and Minnie helped us make the most magical ice cream in the whole world and it would be my pleasure to serve you whatever flavor you'd like." Her eyes lit up like fireworks and she screamed, "May I please have a cookies and cream cone?" I responded, "Of course. Today you are the princess of the Walt Disney World Dolphin." I then offered her parents to select ice cream of their own.

A servant will recognize that serving guests or working with a fellow staff member isn't just about performing a task and fulfilling a job description. Guest service is accomplished with humility, compassion, and all that a spirit of hospitality encompasses. The spirit of hospitality isn't intended to be a reaction to guests' needs. Instead, it's supposed to be a sincere, proactive effort toward building a warm relationship by serving our guests from the heart. A genuine human interaction creates the most powerful, long-lasting service deliverable, which is the vital component in providing a sincere exchange. When we give our best and serve with a spirit of excellence, we continue to grow and develop into valuable assets for our place of employment.

Excellent guest service is an art that can only be performed by someone who understands the spirit of hospitality and walks in it as well. These people have a natural talent to read a guest and proactively deliver. They possess tremendous knowledge of the environment of the establishment in which they serve. They know the menu front and back, forward and backward. They know about local activities, so when a guest asks what they recommend for after-dinner fun, the server has an answer. A solid guest service initiative will always be sure that the service meets or exceeds the guests' expectations.

Genuine guest service is not intended to be a reaction to guests needs. It is simply sincere, proactive effort toward building a warm relationship while serving our guests from the heart.
LARRY STUART HOSPITALITY

Know How to Read People

When we work in guest service, especially bartending, hosting, and waiting tables, we need to know how to read people. Some people like to talk, while others want to be left alone to enjoy their experience. Some will appreciate our sense of humor, while others will find it inappropriate. The spirit of hospitality is invisible. Remember, just enough fun and interaction then walk away. Anyone who wants to succeed in satisfying their guest will need to be able to feel her out and find what will make her experience the best they've ever had.

Knowledge Is Key

Guests expect a positive interaction with a knowledgeable service representative who will meet their needs and beyond. They've chosen to spend their money at your establishment, so they need to feel appreciated and valued in return. Knowing what guests are going to ask—they ask these same questions all the time—and being prepared to answer will make all the difference. We need to have a variety of answers too, because not everyone has the same tastes or enjoys the same activities.

Product knowledge is one of the most important skills our team needs to have. We need to train them to be able to best serve the guest, so they need to know what we have to offer them. They also need to know how the menu items are prepared and cooked, and what the ingredients are, especially with the introduction of gluten-free and other dietary needs/allergies. They need to know what the specials are before they're asked for, whether the special is a dish or on rooms or travel or rentals. When we are able to answer the guests' questions, we're able to provide for their need, which makes the experience much more satisfying for the guest and increases their trust in our ability to serve them.

Another important priority is for our guest service specialists to know where the exciting things are happening in town and how to get to them. Yes, most of our hotels have those lovely brochure racks filled with local attractions, but again, people have different tastes and ideas of what's enjoyable. Not to mention that we'll have families looking for family activities and then we'll have younger couples who want to hit the night club and the older couple who will want to hit the casino. We'll have people who want to visit the commercialized attractions and then we'll have those who would prefer the little-known ones that the locals frequent and consider their best-kept-secret.

Anticipate the Need

The wise guest service provider will be in front of the guests' needs, anticipating them along the way. Our successful execution of our service delivery creates memories that last and builds long-term relationships with our guests. Sometimes this is easy. We can see when a guest's glass is nearly empty, and it's as simple as filling the cup. If we have a family of six checking in, and our rooms come with a standard four-towel set, we can have the housekeeper add a few more to the room prior to our guests' arrival.

But then there are the needs that are more difficult to anticipate. What about food allergies? When a guest comes into our restaurant, how do we know if they're allergic to mushrooms, seafood, peanuts, mustard, or gluten? Some will ask if we have a special menu or may ask us to point out which menu items are free of their allergens. But not all will. Being proactive to ask our guests if they have any allergies or special dietary needs is one way to resolve this challenge. Recognizing that individuals have needs we are unaware of, the spirit of hospitality will always work to consider these in advance.

One of my wife's and my favorite steakhouses is the Capital Grille. The hostess always walks us to our favorite booth, where our tablecloth is pressed, the silverware shines, and there's not a streak or spot on the glasses. The room is clean, and the music is never too loud. Macho, our favorite server, arrives at our table wearing a spotless, pressed white jacket and black tie. He is perfectly groomed—from his clean-cut hair to the shine on his black dress shoes.

What stands out even more is his welcoming smile and positive attitude. He greets us by name, pours our water—making certain mine has no ice—and offers a dish of lemon wedges. He carries a short, sweet, and to-the-point conversation, never talking our ears off. He asks if we would prefer our usual champagne starter or our favorite Malbec varietal.

Notice the detail at this level of service. Our server knows our names, our choice of drink, and that I don't like ice in my water. He has memorized our order, including remembering what we ordered the last time we visited his establishment, which denotes a lasting relationship between server and guest. He anticipates our every need and serves with a spirit of hospitality, which only comes from his heart.

Guest Service Is Invisible

Guest service happens around our clients all the time, but they may never know it's there.

When we operate in the spirit of hospitality, our service instantaneously makes the guest feel welcome and puts them at ease. As soon as they step foot on our property, there should be an immediate sense of comfort and the ability to relax after a long trip or a tiring day of business meetings.

The service Macho provided when my wife and I dined at the Capital Grille was invisible. He engaged with us through the ordering process, and then he never interrupted our conversation. When our guests are dining out on a date, celebrating an anniversary, having a business meeting, or any other important engagement, they should never know our presence unless necessary. Plates should never bang on the table. Refills and requested additions should be delivered gracefully. Invisible service is difficult to detect when our guests are involved in their personal activities. Providing that little extra with our service makes a special difference to our guests.

To Serve Is to Listen

The spirit of hospitality isn't just about the delivery of exceptional service. It's about listening too. We must have two ears and one mouth.

Peter Yesawich's first real job was during the summer between his freshman and sophomore years in college. He was given the opportunity to apprentice with the US sales leader for a European hotel company in New York City, where he spent his days making cold calls to travel agents up and down the east coast to sell them group accommodations in their hotels across the continent. As one would expect, getting past the first person to answer the phone in a busy agency was one of the biggest challenges, so he learned quickly that time spent listening and responding to the concerns of the person who might seem to be the least important in the food chain was time well spent.

Observance of this principle has served him well throughout his career in marketing as he has worked with some of the most well-known and revered brands in the travel industry, such as Disney, Ritz-Carlton, American Express, Mexico, and Bermuda, just to name a few. It has also served him well when nurturing the unique talents of the individuals with whom he has been privileged to work over the years. Each voice on the team is important. Those who desire to contribute deserve to be heard and are entitled to a thoughtful reply—whether or not it aligns with our beliefs or point of view. Because, the most important aspect of any exchange we have with a team member, associate, client or critic is our willingness to give them an opportunity to express *their* point of view. And listen with sincerity.

Guests who feel they have been heard, also feel they have been served. This is a fundamental principle of the spirit of hospitality. Leaders tend to oversell, because they feel their position warrants the final say in the decisions we make. We try to provide our solutions based on what we perceive the guest needs versus what a guest is looking for. "I asked you for the time, not how to build the watch." Sometimes, we like to listen to the wonderful sound of our own voice rather than listening to the need of our guests. Instead, we need to place ourselves in the shoes of the person who is seeking our service. This is critical in order to serve them above and beyond all they could ask or think. In turn, this makes our guest feel valued and appreciated.

Providing the Wow Factor in Every Experience

Ritz-Carlton. Starbucks. Walt Disney World Magic Kingdom. Outback Steakhouse. The Hilton. Southwest Airlines. Marriot. Chick-fil-A. Most people will recognize these names, and they will immediately conjure an image of something distinct about each one. Whether it's the smile on the face of the person who greets them, the taste of a particular culinary experience, the comfort of a room, or any other facet of their experience with an establishment, the guest knows what to expect when they walk in the door. The question is, does your staff serve your brand with passion and purpose?

One of the first things we need to do when creating a spirit of hospitality is focus on the brand. Is everything we're doing within the company supporting the brand? This is important, because If we take care of the brand, the brand will take care of us. If we focus on the company first, the company thrives. People get promotions, new stores are established, and the company continues to grow. As satisfied guests alert others to the care they received while at our establishment, our name becomes recognized by more and more people. And eventually, hopefully, our company's name is going to be recognized internationally. Or it isn't. What can we do to make it so?

1. Be extraordinary, not ordinary.
2. Enhance the guest's experience.
3. Be on top of your game.
4. Appreciate the guest's loyalty.
5. Build strong relationships.

Overall, our main goal should be to provide that wow factor for every guest who visits us. The Ritz Carlton has this ability hands down.

In June of 2017, a family friend graduated from college. To celebrate, she and her father visited the Ritz Carlton in San Francisco, California. Prior to their visit, the director of guest services contacted Jeff by phone, inquiring about the reason for their trip to San Francisco. "Are you celebrating anything special?" she asked. When he told her that they were celebrating his daughter's graduation, she asked for her name. To their surprise and delight, upon their arrival, they discovered a custom-made chocolate dessert spelling out *Congratulations for Your Graduation, Brittany*, a bottle of Champaign, fruit, balloons, and more awaiting them in their suite. Their expectations were blown away. This is the Ritz Carlton Gold Standard—their special version of the spirit of hospitality. Every time anyone in our family stays with them, we are wowed. They live up to their brand. Their internal guests behave as one would expect ladies and gentlemen to behave, and they treat their external guests like they are ladies and gentlemen as well.

TAKEOUT:

▸ Serve your brand by providing excellent guest service.
▸ When we walk out our establishment's culture, our guests notice and will spread the word about how they felt welcomed and at home while visiting us.

Do the right things for the right reasons and you get the right results.
(Right Things + Right Reasons = Right Results)

LARRY STUART HOSPITALITY

13

Conflict and the Spirit of Hospitality

Statistics suggest that when guests complain, business owners and leaders ought to get excited about it. The complaining guest represents a huge opportunity for more business.

- ZIG ZIGLAR

O ne day, I was driving down the road in McAfee, New Jersey, and as I came around a curve, the guy coming the other way started yelling and pointing like I was doing something wrong. As I passed him, he called out, "Pig! Pig! Pig!" Huh. What did I do to deserve being called a pig? Or maybe he was trying to tell me a cop was around the bend. Not a nice way to refer to the police.

As I rounded the curve, what did I find? An actual pig was standing in the middle of the road.

When I saw the pig, I realized the guy was warning me versus calling me a name. I had to swerve off the road and ended up hitting a tree in order to avoid hitting the pig. When our perception is skewed, we end up in that proverbial tree because we missed the warning.

Find the Truth in Every Communication

Perception can be a devious thing. In this age of technology with text messages and emails, social media posts, and so many more ways to communicate without a phone or a person standing in front of us, it's too easy to misunderstand what someone is saying or the tone he or she is saying it in. Which can open up a whole can of worms we don't want spoiling our recipe for the spirit of hospitality. It's important to realize that how we perceive things isn't necessarily how the person who delivered the message intended us to receive it. Sometimes, before we react, we need to be proactive.

Quality communication will promote change and better relations. This turns around hidden agendas and misconceptions, stimulating productivity. Which is why knowing how to effectively communicate is important. A skilled communicator is aware of the tone of his or her words and always makes eye contact. Knowing how to read body language and recognizing how it affects our interactions is also key.

If our business partner sends us a message, and it strikes a chord in us as being offensive or disconcerting, we need to take a moment or even a day before responding. Haste doesn't help in this situation. Instead, consider the person who has sent the message. Is this normal behavior or attitude for him? No? Then it probably wasn't his intent to come across the way we're perceiving it.

If the message is unclear, there's never any harm in following the next step of effective communication. Respond with, "If I'm hearing you correctly, you're saying…" Repeat the message back to the sender. This gives him the opportunity to clarify any points or tones we may have missed or misunderstood. And it gives us the opportunity to respond without embarrassing ourselves by overreacting to nothing. We have an opportunity to operate in the spirit of hospitality, which doesn't judge. It clarifies.

This communication technique works as well in person:

1. Sender speaks or sends message electronically.

2. Receiver hears the message. Receiver repeats what has been said back to Sender.
3. Sender clarifies what needs clarification.
4. Receiver receives clarification and responds accordingly.

When we operate in all the ingredients of the spirit of hospitality, there is very little room for error, and simple communication leaves little room for misunderstanding. What happens when we disagree with the sender? Or the receiver disagrees with us? That's an opportunity for discussion, a learning experience, and living with others with understanding—despite our differences. As individuals with unique gifts, talents, perspectives, likes, dislikes, and so much more, we must learn to respect others and their individuality, loving them for who they are first. It's only once someone knows how much we care that they'll care how much we know. It's only then they'll trust enough and be willing to receive a lesson or learn something new from us.

In the story about the pig that I shared above, my perception went straight to what I would consider the obvious. Either he was offended by something I'd done, he was calling me a name, or there were cops nearby and he didn't like them based on the slur he was using. Only the truth was more obvious than my perception, which was skewed. The truth was, there was a pig in the road. We need to be about the business of seeking out the truth in every communication while realizing every individual has their own unique perspective.

Overcome Offenses

We've all had challenging days before. The alarm goes off too early after a rough night of sleep, a spouse wakes up cranky, a child does not finish their chores. We're late for work. Caught in traffic. Things just aren't going well. Maybe someone we know received a diagnosis or we were notified a loved one had passed. Maybe the car had a flat tire, the washing machine quit, and the savings account is empty. Life happens—both the good and the challenging. So, when a guest or co-worker comes to me with a negative attitude, I have to take their day into consideration. What has happened to set them off? Remember, most guest complaints—internal and external—are sincere, legitimate, realistic, and warranted.

I worked at a first-class hotel where we had gathered in the ballrooms for a wedding with 575 guests. The atmosphere buzzed with excitement, and we were about to watch the bride and groom enter for their reception when a bellhop ran in to retrieve me. "We have a situation in the lobby."

I nodded as we left the noise of the reception and took off running for the lobby. Breathless, I arrived to find that a middle-aged man threatened a bewildered front-desk agent for making him wait two hours for a room that had been promised an early check in. To top that off, I overheard him telling her that his spa day had been reserved weeks in advance, but when he checked it online during his flight there, the reservation had disappeared as if he'd never placed it.

This gentleman needed immediate attention from a leader. I approached with my hands out. "Sir, may I be of assistance?"

With a scowl on his reddened face, he asked, "Who are you?"

"I'm Larry Stuart, sir. The manager. How can I provide positive assistance?"

He firmed himself and spewed his frustration while I caught my breath. "Your staff is incompetent. How difficult is it for the housekeepers to have a room ready before the guests arrive? You knew I was coming early, and everyone I spoke with guaranteed me that room would be ready for an early arrival."

Recognizing that his words could destroy our relationship with the guests who lingered in our lobby, I invited him to my office.

He wasn't budging. "Oh no! Everyone here," he gestured toward our guests, who gawked at his brashness, "can hear just how lousy your service really is."

My front desk agent rounded the counter and handed me his VIP card and invoice. I scanned it and noted his request to have flowers waiting in the room with a bottle of champagne. He and his wife were celebrating their twenty-fifth wedding anniversary. I took a look around the room to see if she was present. I assumed she was the lady sitting on a nearby couch with her head buried in her hands. I needed to take immediate action.

"Sir, I'm truly sorry for what has transpired. I promise you this is a most unusual circumstance and not what our service stands for. Would you allow me the opportunity to provide resolution, restitution, and peace? Please bring your wife, and let's go to my office. I'd like to see what we can do to make this the grandest weekend you've ever had in our city."

He heaved a sigh before taking his VIP card, which I offered him. Grumbling under his breath, he gathered his wife and followed me to the office.

I nodded my approval for the front-desk agent to take action. By the time I had the guests comfortably seated in my office with ice water in their hands, the agent had upgraded them to the honeymoon suite—a five-hundred-dollar-per-night upgrade—and booked for a relaxing spa day followed by a romantic dinner at one of the best restaurants in town overlooking the pool and waterfall. Meanwhile, my bellman brought their luggage to their room and left flowers and champagne on ice, along with a signed note from our guest service staff, on the table.

In the end, we exceeded his expectations. He knew that we truly cared and wanted him to have an incredible weekend with his wife. Despite the fact that I no longer work for that hotel, our relationship continues to this day. He returns to that property on a regular basis and recommends their services to others.

Guest Service Recovery

The integrity of a true service-oriented business is how they respond when things go wrong. And things will go wrong multiple times every day. It's how well we provide our service recovery that separates us from the competition. When we're in service-recovery mode, it's difficult to turn the guest around. We've already established that we weren't reliable in fulfilling their felt needs. We've already dropped the ball, and now it's time to recover it before we lose the guest entirely—and their advertising about our establishment turns negative. We have the opportunity to win a guest for life through our guest service recovery. If done right, the guest will tell all their friends about their awesome experience at our establishment and will bring their friends or business back with them the next time they visit us. We are now going to do everything we can to rectify the situation. If we always try to model a professional servant, addressing the issues at hand to cure the challenges while defusing the temperament of the angry guest, we will often win them over. This requires sincerity, empathy, and kindness. We must always remember to take a servant's humble attitude when executing guest service recovery, keeping our demeanor professional as we respond to our guests' challenges.

> *How people treat you is their story; how you react is yours.*
> **- WAYNE DYER**

Our goal is service recovery. Providing restitution may be as easy as passing a slice of apple pie a la mode after a challenging meal, upgrading an airline ticket, or offering a gift card for use locally or upon a return visit. Reponses may also be costly, such as providing a free weekend at our hotel or resort or offering a free flight after multiple cancellations due to mechanical failures.

Sometimes it's the smaller gestures that make the greatest impact. When we take the time to handwrite a card rather than send an email, make a phone call rather than text, or speak to the person rather than sending the front-desk agent in place of the leader, it makes an impression upon the guest that could lead to a lasting relationship.

In guest service recovery mode, we must honor the Golden Rule: Love your neighbor as yourself. When we treat others with respect and kindness, they respond in like kind.

The most important message for us to communicate to our guest is that they are the most important part of our day. Their relationship must be appreciated. When things go wrong, our service recovery is what will resound with them, so be sure it says we value them. This will keep them coming back to our business for years to come. We must build the relationship.

1. **Stay calm.** Under all circumstances the staff must maintain their self-control and professional manner. This is business, and it's all about turning around our guest. We cannot take this exchange, in any way, as personal. Remember, all eyes are on us as much as they're on the antagonist. People will remember how we resolved a heated situation, which should turn into repeat business.

2. **Listen carefully.** We must teach our staff to hear what the guest is saying, allowing them to vent. We do not want to interrupt them or tune them out. Train them to ask questions that show their concern for the other person. "It sounds like you're upset, so please allow me to provide a resolution. How can I be of assistance?" or "It would be my pleasure to discuss this further with you. May I invite you into my office?" When asking someone how they're doing, be sure you mean it and are ready to listen for their answer, using the communication skills we discussed in the previous section. Make the person aware that you hear their frustration. Show that you are sincere and empathetic. If you're having a difficult time understanding their frustration, put yourself in their shoes. If they aren't willing to talk, at least they may calm down enough to gain the entry needed in order to resolve the situation. Remember that they need you to turn around their negative predicament. Use your time, words, and strategy wisely.

3. **Empathize.** Train your staff to see the situation from the guest's point of view. I have always believed that taking the high road brings us through life's greatest challenges. Kindness always wins in the end. A guest can be screaming at the top of their lungs, berating you in front of your fellow peers and insulting you personally. The only course of action for you is to use wisdom. Be quick to listen, slow to speak, and do not respond with anger. Responding in a calm professional manner is taking the high road.

It's putting yourself in the guest's shoes and understanding how we would feel if we were them. We'd be irate, too, if someone had messed up our anniversary trip through lack of follow-through on promises made. Our word is gold. We must let our yes be yes and our no be no. Otherwise, we lose the trust of our guests.

4. **Avoid becoming defensive.** Train your staff not to take complaints personally or feel threatened. They are on the same side, confronting the problem together with you. Granted, there are times when we need to take responsibility for our actions and words. I'm not talking about that. I'm talking about getting offended because someone else is not on their game. Joy comes from within us. It isn't based on our circumstances. Happiness is what requires us to be influenced by outside sources. Someone can be angry with us and leave us upset or angry in return. But that person can't steal our joy—unless we allow them to. Don't take their offense personally. If we need to admit we've done or said something wrong, confess and ask forgiveness. But if we weren't the ones to blame, don't take on their negative attitude. Again, it may be time to take the high road and walk away. Never stoop to someone's lower standard. I have always shared my positive enthusiasm with those around me. It's who I am. There are others who choose to do the opposite. It's a choice. Servants take the high road.

5. **Accept responsibility.** Guests aren't interested in excuses and explanations. Team members should accept responsibility for solving the problem. Figure out what the root of the problem is. We don't want to deal with the surface issue, because that won't resolve anything. That would be like putting a Band-Aid on a wound that requires stitches. Find out what is at the deepest point of the issue so it can be taken care of. "What has happened? What would resolve your situation?"

6. **Work to find a solution.** Ask how the guest would like to see it resolved. Not everyone will have the same answer. Let's say you've

sent a meal to a table, and the steak was cooked medium but the guest's idea of medium is well-done. One guest may suck it up and eat the meat as it is, grimacing with every chew—have you picked up on their body language, reading the guest—while another will point out the mistake. At which point, you'll apologize and reorder the steak. The guest may be satisfied that simply. However, another person may be irritable and want a free meal. Find out what the guest desires in order to make it right for them as an individual. This emphasizes that we care about the people who support our business or work alongside us. If this doesn't resolve the issue, it may be time to involve a third party, such as the chef or manager.

7. **Follow up.** Be sure the guest is satisfied with the solution. Check back with the table to be sure to qualify that their expectations have been met and that everything is now okey. When the guest checks out of the hotel, follow up by asking if they enjoyed their stay. It's always appropriate to ask if there's anything further we can do for our guests.

Many operations fail due to guest service specialists who don't know their job or how to solve guest issues. Research indicates that ninety-six percent of unhappy guests never complain about rude or discourteous treatment. What they typically do is not return. To top that off, with today's social media access, as many as 300 people will hear about a bad service experience at our establishment. We must train our staff—and do so consistently—in order to beat or eliminate the odds of this happening. After coaching countless crew members throughout my career, the one fact that I can hang my hat on is that tough guests always provide the sharpening to our guest service skill sets and feed us exactly what we need to continuously take the high road while learning how to interact with that irate individual by providing the spirit of hospitality.

Leaders, keep yourself informed.

▸ You can find the cause of the challenge, and keep it from happening again.

▸ You can ensure that the challenge has been handled to the guest's satisfaction by checking with them before they leave the restaurant.

▸ Treat guest complaints as opportunities to win back their loyalty.

▸ Team members must notify the leader of all complaints—even if the challenge has already been solved.

▸ Teach team members to approach guests to follow up on complaints to assure they have been handled to the guest's satisfaction.

When we are willing to take the guest's concerns into consideration, we calm the guest down and demonstrate our professional demeanor. Guests will recognize our positive attitude through our willingness to listen and providing a solution, especially when we aren't looking to engage defensively, stooping to their level of argumentative behavior. Our kind words can quickly turn away the guest's wrath. We need to handle the wants and needs profitably for both the guest and ourselves, keeping in mind that the guest is always right, even when he's wrong.

Internal Conflict

What if the struggle is with someone we work with or are related to? Bosses, team members, and co-workers aren't immune to having challenging days, and trivial matters can easily set people off. When someone loses it, there are several ways to handle the situation. Breathe. Count to ten. Excuse yourself from the situation. Walk away. Ultimately, we can use the same tactics we would use with our external guests. Let the person know how much they're cared for, ask if there's anything you can do to help, and work to resolve the issue by implementing the spirit of hospitality. I've always found joy in improving someone's day, and that's our goal with guest service recovery. It's that simple.

It's important to note that there is a time and a place to deal with internal conflict. It's *not* on the floor, in front of guests. As leaders, it's best to invite the team members off the floor and take them into the office or another quiet place out of earshot of guests and others. Stay calm at all times. It's a servant leader's role to set the tone for resolution. Again, if we allow our own emotions to override our position, we won't accomplish our objective—responding to and redirecting the differences between our crew members.

Seat them and ask what's going on. The goal is to neutralize and discover the facts by getting to the truth of the matter. We want to avoid third party involvement and gossip at all costs. Fair treatment of all parties involved is a key in these situations. As leaders and mediators, we must listen first, then ask questions. Give each team member the benefit of the doubt. Then speak individually with all of the parties involved. Too often we jump to conclusions. "Sally said this..." Did she really? Or did the receiver hear it wrong and relay it in a way that would make Peter assume she meant something she didn't? We can't assume we know what either team member said or meant during their disagreement. Instead, we must find out what happened and decide what to do to rectify the situation once we've gathered enough information to do so fairly. If our culture is rich with the spirit of hospitality, the outcome shouldn't even be questioned.

Once we've learned the details of the situations, we need to attempt to build up and encourage the team members. If they are still edgy, respond accordingly. If they need time off to refocus, allow it. Better to let them take the day than cost the establishment business. Most of the time, the team members will only need a few moments—maybe a fifteen-minute break—to blow off steam and get their smile back. Keep in mind that we all go through storms in life. That's a moment for grace and maybe some extra time off while the team member sorts things out. But beware of the high maintenance person who needs more time away from work than is necessary, thus prohibiting productivity. My friend Edie Melson put it well when she said, "Kindness isn't nice." Sometimes, we must be firm in our correction. If they cannot receive our correction or resolve their conflict, they may need to reconsider their choice of workplace. We are running a business, and we must adhere to our standards of responsibility and accountability to our operation. It's a privilege to work for our establishment, and we are not running a daycare for unprofessional individuals.

We are human, we have emotions, and we have days. We aren't machines that can easily be programmed. Our team members don't come with manuals. It's up to us, as leaders, to remain open to working through a variety of situations and circumstances with them while maintaining an environment with professional boundaries. Every team member will need personal attention, as we are all unique in how we operate, interact, and respond. There will be no blanket solutions for managing individuals. Servant leaders know what's best in every circumstance because we've been in their position and understand that at the end of the day, the buck stops with us. We understand fairness and justice. Wisdom, experience, and commitment to providing consistent operations need to take over in these situations.

Mistakes Aren't the End of the World

Challenging days aren't the only thing that bring issues. We've all made mistakes. It's how we learn. And just because we've made a mistake doesn't mean we're a failure. It means something didn't work out, but it's not the end of the world. Failure is life's greatest teacher. The question is, how well do we handle others' mistakes or failures? We need to be able to recognize that other people are as human as we are. How would we want to be treated if we made a mistake? Would we want to be taken to task on it or to be told how much of a failure we are? Or would we want support from our mentor or leader? If we don't like being chided for our shortcomings, we shouldn't treat others in that manner either. It's the age-old adage: Do unto others what you would want done unto you. Extend the spirit of hospitality.

Every one of us has been offended at some point in time, although it seems some get over being hurt easier or faster than others. Have you ever wondered how they do it? It starts with a compassionate heart. Each time we pick ourselves up, recovering gets easier. In the process, we develop character, self-worth, and resilience. It ends with forgiveness.

What do we do when we are the ones offended? We can opt to hold a grudge, treat one another poorly in response to poor treatment, and any number of other unhealthy coping mechanisms. These options tend to lead to bitterness and resentment toward the person who has offended us. They don't have to, though. Holding bitterness against another person is like taking the poison for them. It does no harm to them while it eats us alive from the inside out. The only antidote is understanding and forgiveness.

Many misunderstand forgiveness to mean admitting that the offender wasn't guilty of their offense. This is not true. Forgiveness doesn't forget or excuse the offense. It frees us to move past it. And it offers the offender a second chance to do the right thing. Will they? Who knows? When we've done all that we know to do to improve a situation and the other person is no longer receptive to our efforts, it's time to dust off our hands and walk away. Take the higher ground. Make peace the priority. There's no need to be their doormat. There's far more to life than the present moment. Get past it. We have others to serve.

Be proactive. Have a plan in place as to how you will deal with those who are having a challenging day, have made a mistake, or have caused an offense. Once you've developed your plan, stick to it. When handling these situations, remember to do so with compassion. It doesn't take anything but courage to offer team support, a word of encouragement, or a simple smile.

The Power of a Positive Attitude

PACE: Positive Action Changes Everything
– LARRY STUART HOSPITALITY

Attitude is the way we perceive and approach life. It's the lens we see life through. My parents instilled in me the message that my attitude would be directly responsible for the outcome of everything I touched. The quality of my life would depend entirely on the attitude I took. If our attitude has a positive focus, our relationships will be fruitful, we will be resourceful at doing our jobs, and our life will be valuable. Having a positive attitude will always attract the right people to team with us in bringing a successful initiative and result through everything we are associated with. A positive spirit should be our calling card, not a fallback plan.

In his book *How to Win Friends and Influence People*, Dale Carnegie wrote, "You can always get ahead by being positive, especially in challenging and negative situations." Negativity rolls off the back of a positive person. She is rarely knocked off balance by the circumstances surrounding her, because she understands that joy is something that comes from within, and no one can take it from her unless she allows them to. Someone else's challenging day isn't going to negatively affect hers. She rises above and steps into the role of encourager. Everyone wants to be in her company, because she increases the quality of the lives around her. Positive attitudes are contagious.

That attitude turnaround may not be as easy for others as it is for our friend in the paragraph above. Did you know that you can change your attitude by using certain actions to regulate your personal feelings? It requires a little creativity on our part, but when we focus on speaking positive words and performing acts of kindness, our outlook on life will become lighter, and our work will become easier. We're more easily motivated when our words and tone of voice are pleasant toward others. In order to turn a negative into a positive, we must lighten up and create a positive attitude. *Create* is the key.

To defy the law of gravity, airplanes need lift. Lift takes a plane off the ground and gets us where we need to go. In the workplace, we can fly as high as we want to when the spirit of hospitality is our lift. The spirit of hospitality can propel our team above the gravity of negativity and bring us into a space where we can do the right thing—for ourselves, our team, and our guests. Every contact with a fellow worker or guest should be a special event. It must be positive. When this occurs, we have accomplished a successful guest service delivery.

TAKEOUT:

▸ Conflicts will happen. People will make mistakes.
▸ The key is to be proactive rather than reactive.
▸ Have a plan for how to handle conflict in the workplace and with guests. Make sure everyone knows what is expected ahead of time.
▸ As a leader, be certain to take the lead in these situations. Find the truth. Manage the issue.

Treat everyone you meet with politeness,
kindness, and compassion.
LARRY STUART HOSPITALITY

14

Kindness

I've learned that people will forget what you said, people will forget what you did, but people will never forget how you made them feel.
- MAYA ANGELOU

Kindness is the language of the heart. It starts within one person and is evidenced in how they respond to others. A smile. A gentle tone. Eye contact when spoken to. These are all easy enough to do, but we often have difficulty maintaining kindness. The moment our day starts to go south, we lose the smile, avoid eye contact, and snap when someone wants to have a conversation. We want to isolate rather than participate.

In order to maintain a spirit of kindness, one must first remember the golden rule: Treat others as you would like to be treated. When I was growing up, my parents always demonstrated an appropriate way to treat others. Parents teach their children manners, wholesome values, and to treat others fairly and with kindness. This way of bringing up children who can put others before themselves has gotten lost as violence and mistrust have crept into society. That's not to say no one raises decent, respectful citizens anymore. There are plenty who do, but it's rarer than it was sixty or seventy years ago.

Acts of kindness should be a regular part of daily life. We should always be aware of those around us and be on the lookout for opportunities to do something nice for someone else, whether it's paying for the person in line behind us, saying a kind word or complementing our neighbor, offering a word of encouragement to a co-worker, or stopping to help someone change their tire. In reality, these things only take a few seconds or minutes out of our day. Most times, it doesn't take much to be a good Samaritan. Unfortunately, so many of us are too busy to look up and notice others' needs, instead focusing on our own and what we must accomplish in a day.

We have the potential to influence others to respond in like manner. Have you ever been in line at a grocery store and had another guest offer to pay for your order? Doesn't that warm your heart and make you want to do the same? I've been in the drive-through line at Starbucks when the person at the window has said the pay-it-forward movement has been going on for at least thirty guests. One person decided to pay for someone's latte, and thirty cars later, people were still following suit. It doesn't take but one person to start something good. It's also just as easy for one person to start something evil. If only more people were willing to start something good.

No matter how large or small our role, we're all contributing to the larger story unfolding within our lives, businesses, and organizations. The question is, what are we sowing into those areas? Because what we're sowing will directly affect what we reap. If we sow good seeds in freshly tilled soil, we should be able to reap a full harvest. But if we choose to sow bad seeds or sow good seeds in bad soil, we shouldn't expect the harvest to be good. Our choices will determine the outcome in every situation in our lives, and we need to be mature enough to accept that and wise enough to make the right, responsible decisions. What we reap will depend directly on how and where we sow.

Once we've decided to sow the seeds in the good soil, the work doesn't end when the seeds go into the ground. Sowing requires an investment. The garden must be tended throughout the growth process. The plants need water, fertilizer, and protection from damaging factors such as too much sunlight, weeds, and insects and animals. We must maintain an environment in which the seed can thrive as it grows to produce the life-giving fruit. If we let the garden go, the damaging factors will overcome it, and the crop will die before it yields the fruit.

Just as we do in our garden, we need to be aware of what we sow in our homes, workplaces, and social environments. When things are going crazy at work with deadlines, disruptions, emergencies, setbacks, and back-to-back meetings, how do we handle the pressure? Does it overwhelm us? Do we dream of the day it all clears and work can go back to normal? Do we ignore the issues and hope they will resolve themselves? Or do we face them head on? Because issues, like weeds, won't just go away. It takes plucking and sometimes digging to remove them. And if we ignore them, they overtake the crop, enveloping the good with the bad.

We all have a responsibility to our creator, ourselves, and those who depend on us. When we cannot serve them with joy, kindness, and integrity, we stunt not only our own growth, but theirs as well. We need to sow these things into our lives regardless of which area of life we're dealing with in the moment. Because we will reap what we sow.

My mom always said, "Goodness brings goodness." When we do the right thing for the right reasons, it always comes back to bless us in the end. So, what does good sowing and good reaping look like? It looks like developing quality relationships with one another by treating each other with kindness and respect, putting others before ourselves. It involves being sincere both in our intentions and in our actions as we walk in the spirit of hospitality. When we need to bring correction, we need to do it with consideration for others, enabling our criticisms to be constructive rather than destructive. Then and only then will we reap the goodness we so desire.

TAKEOUT:

▸ I think people have forgotten the value of being kind.

▸ A kind act or word has the power to make someone feel great.

▸ The value of kindness speaks the truth about a person's self-worth.

▸ When we act in kindness, the recipient is made to feel exceptional, important, and special.

▸ Kindness is something we don't soon forget. And that is something the guest who enters your establishment needs to feel as soon as they step foot through the door until the moment they leave. Otherwise, they may not ever come back.

Humility fuels the spirit of hospitality.
LARRY STUART HOSPITALITY

15

Humility

The best way to find yourself is to lose yourself in the service of others.
- GHANDI

M y father, Enzo Stuarti, a natural tenor, toured with greats such as Jerry Lewis, Sammy Davis, Bob Hope, and Milton Berle. One time, my mother had to leave the theater to get something from our car. When she returned and couldn't open the backstage door, she went around to the front and got in line with hundreds of people who were coming to see the show. She never went to the front of the line and told the theater staff who she was and who she was with. Instead, she practiced humility, not putting herself above others as if she were someone who deserved special treatment. This is what a humble spirit looks like.

The Spirit of Hospitality can't be executed without possessing the secret ingredient of humility. Without humility, one cannot understand a heart of service. When humility is at the heart of our intentions and motivations, the spirit of hospitality acts naturally through kindness, a servant's heart, and keeping others first. This is where true purpose and service come together in achieving the greatest gift of giving instead of giving just to get something in return, whether that's accolade or reward.

Many often mistake humility for weakness. This is not the case. Humility is all about putting oneself before others. It's a strength, not a weakness. One cannot live a life of service without being humble.

There's no room for pride or selfishness within the hospitality industry. When those are present, life is all about me, and the person I'm serving moves into second place in my life. Without humility, we simply cannot understand the heart of service. Serving involves catering to others' needs without emphasizing how great we are or needing someone else to tell us the same.

While I was achieving my bachelor of science degree at Cornell's School of Hotel and Restaurant Administration, Robert Beck was the acting dean. Dean Beck fully operated in the spirit of hospitality. He was a humble servant leader with a sincere passion for growing students into leaders. He watched over us like a proud father, and he reveled in his students' successes. He always put others before himself, and others felt accomplished, important, and necessary when they were around him.

A person in Dean Beck's position is typically difficult to reach. But he made himself available to his students, and when I was just getting started in my education, he took me under his wing. He guided my scholastic steps, helped me find internships, and directed my career like a professional who truly cared for others. He was the epitome of a humble man.

Responsible Stewardship

A steward is someone who actively directs affairs, whether those affairs are financial, relational, or have to do with providing food and beverages to a large group of people. Great stewards are responsible and humble. They make no excuses for their shortcomings and are honest with those who they serve. They also want the best for them, because they put others' needs before their own, making sure to accomplish the tasks before them with diligence and excellence. Their humility involves transparency with others, which leads to accountability. Regardless of our roles, we are all stewards over something—even ourselves.

The first thing we are stewards over is our own gifts and talents. For those of us in the hospitality industry, these talents would be such things as the joy we experience in the kitchen, whether practicing the culinary arts or washing dishes. Maybe you are outgoing and love to meet new people, so you serve tables or work the front desk at a hotel. Either way, your gift of hospitality is part of your DNA, and tapping into it so easy you could do it in your sleep. Good stewards share their gifts and talents by serving others.

The second thing we are stewards over is our time. This can look like many things in the hospitality industry. Do we save steps—not to take shortcuts, but to manage our time well and multiply the effectiveness of our service? Do we get enough sleep at night so we can perform at our best productivity level the next day? As leaders, do we manage our administrative duties well so we can be on the floor with our team during peak hours and interact with our guests? When we properly steward our time, our guest service delivery should flow seamlessly.

The third thing we are stewards over is our finances. One thing to consider in this area of stewardship is whether or not a company would want you managing their finances based on how you manage your own. Granted there are many who live paycheck to paycheck in today's world, but what are you doing with those paychecks? Are you hoarding your money, forgetting the blessings attached to giving? Are you a disorganized procrastinator when it comes to being responsible for paying your bills because you can't help but buy that new suit or expensive handbag when you get your next paycheck? Or maybe you're excellent at finances and have all your ducks in a row. Your bills are paid in a timely manner. You have an emergency reserve fund and are investing in your retirement and your kids' college account. The ultimate question is, would you hire yourself to manage someone else's finances? Because in a way, when we work for another person or a company, that's what we're doing. Our ability to fulfill our responsibility in our positions will determine the happiness of our company's clients, resulting in a financial increase or decrease.

We are also the master of whatever we are able to accomplish and those things we don't accomplish. We are responsible for our results. Our destiny is entirely determined by how hard and smart we work to achieve our goals. If we are truly passionate about our career path and we learn from the ground up, we will one day find ourselves positioned in a leadership role or earning that raise while exceeding our goals.

As stewards, we need to view a life of service as a responsibility. In doing so, we can take on an entirely different attitude or approach as to how we serve others. My mom always used to tell me to keep my feet on the ground and keep my head out of the clouds. When I was prideful, others came second, and I reaped the consequences of the attitudes and choices I had sown. When I finally realized she was right and that others deserved my attention, kindness, and service, I immediately began walking in the blessings she'd predicted.

Respect for Others

In my late twenties, I transitioned from the entertainment industry into the hospitality industry. I loved being in front of people on stage. Which is probably why God decided I needed to be parked in the hospitality industry for forty-plus years. I needed to learn to serve others and to submit to authority, even when—in some cases—I knew more about my role and the projects than my leaders did. I wasn't going to be in the spotlight or the one getting the applause anymore. Now, it was going to be about everyone else but me.

Thankfully, I had mentors like Phil Pistilli to help me become a humble servant, keep my mouth shut, and learn from others. I always had an entrepreneurial mindset, which made it difficult for me to take orders from others. I knew how things worked and could see ways to improve on systems already in place. When I became the food and beverage leader at one of Phil's properties, the Raphael Hotel, I had to work under a leader who didn't know my job as well as I did. One day, Phil pulled me aside and reamed me out. "It's important to learn to work with a leader that you don't agree with, because you'll learn more from that situation than you will from any other." It was time for me to humble myself and respect those in authority over me. This was such a difficult transition for me.

Not much later, I would land a job with the Walt Disney World Dolphin. Would you believe me if I said I didn't want to work with that leader either? How about if I told you he became my best friend?

Sooner or later, we'll all end up working with people who are tough bosses. Rather than allow that to rub us the wrong way, we should take the opportunity to learn from the situation. It helps shape our skill set and self-discipline, and it helps us grow so we can better glean from their leadership style and capabilities.

On the other side of the floor, as leaders, we need to recognize that we cannot demand respect. Respect is something commanded, not demanded. We command respect by treating others with the same. When someone sees that we respect them as a person, for who they are, with the gifts and talents they've been given ... as well as their flaws, they are far more likely to demonstrate respect toward us in return. Respect is given when we treat others with kindness, compassion, and encouragement. Demanding respect puts up a wall between a leader and their entire team. If we want resistance, demanding respect is a great way to get it. Humility recognizes that respect is earned and strives to treat others with the same respect we desire to gain.

Admitting Mistakes

One of the most difficult things in life is to admit our personal flaws. Each of us has them, so what's the big deal? It's as if admitting our mistakes, that we're wrong, or that we're weak in an area will be the end of us. Maybe we fear judgment or inferiority. But if we can never admit to our shortcomings, we can never grow beyond them.

We are the master of our mistakes. When we make a mistake, we immediately need to own it, admit it, and make any necessary apology that goes with it. As mentioned before, we're accountable for handling the affairs of others, and if we drop the ball or make a mistake, we need to remedy it before we quickly fall into the temptation to be deceitful, which leads down the wrong path. Having a humble spirit allows us to admit when we're wrong and offer the apology without being concerned about what others will think or how they will respond. Remember, we're only responsible for our own actions and reactions. The high road is the only alternative.

This ability to admit to our mistakes is also a form of accountability. We always answer to someone higher than us. Children answer to parents. Students answer to teachers. Team members answer to leaders. Team leaders answer to stakeholders. At the same time, others are accountable to us. Not everyone appreciates this concept, but that doesn't diminish its truth. We are all responsible for our decisions—not our parents, teachers, siblings, spouse, boss, co-workers, or friends. When we make mistakes, we need to own up to them, not hide them or try to blame them on someone else.

Have you ever been at the water cooler at work and overheard someone complaining about someone else? "James doesn't do half the work I do. How is it he's getting the promotion?" Maybe they complained about the boss. "Who does he think he is telling me I need to up my game or I'll be fired? Has he been here during the dinner rush in the past six months? It doesn't help that we ran out of fish." I'm willing to bet you could find plenty wrong with your workplace, but have you considered that you could be an agent of change if you started with yourself? We must live as positive examples, sowing seeds of reinforcement into our environments.

We should be in the habit of assessing ourselves by taking a regular inventory of our heart, intentions, and performances. Conviction alerts us to anything in our lives that stands against our valued principles. The key to submitting to that conviction and overcoming whatever may be holding us back is to admit we need to change in the first place. I had to look inside myself and realize that I needed to put others first if I was ever going to grow beyond my pride and disrespect for authorities.

Once we can admit we need to change some aspect of our life, we're able to take the next step toward change. For me, that looked like getting out and working. My goal was to grow in my positions and learn as much as I could about the hospitality industry in a rapid period of time. I would become engaged with my work and my co-workers and my team leaders.

I longed to work with first-class operators, like Phil, who would be willing to take me under their wing and teach me the ins and outs of our business. I set out to prove my salt anywhere I worked, which meant working twelve to fifteen hours per day, seven days a week. Not because it was about the money. It wasn't. A hard-work ethic is what made the difference in me, humbling me. Once I did these things, I noticed the changes occurring in my life, and they brought maturity and selflessness with them.

When we take the time to make the difference in ourselves, we bring that talent, experience, and intent to the table and are able to offer a hotel chain, airline, restaurant, or any other place of business something valuable. People will take note of the difference in us and become curious as to how they can have the same experiences. It's then we'll begin to see that because of the spirit of hospitality operating in us, we have the ability to affect change in the world around us.

The Teachable Spirit

Movies and television often portray corporate leaders as selfish, ruthless people who will do whatever it takes to get ahead, no matter who else gets hurt. In real life, though, successful leaders are hard-nosed when it's necessary, but they are not arrogant. They understand that they don't know everything, and they are open-minded enough to look for opportunities to continue learning each day. An efficient leader gives others the same respect he or she expects to receive and recognizes that no job in the company is beneath him or her, whether it's making the morning coffee or even cleaning an occasional restroom. The spirit of hospitality isn't connected to a job description or paycheck. It's part of our DNA. Leaders who are humble recognize they still have much to learn.

One of the keys of humility is being able to acknowledge that we don't always know everything. Being able to ask for help is imperative to having a humble spirit. Lifelong learners are wise people. They are able to identify when they are struggling with a concept or need further training in a particular area. They search out mentors and accept apprenticeships in order to learn new skills and further their careers or develop their character. One will either learn from the best, work for the best, and be their best or they'll struggle through life, never experiencing what could have been.

I would caution you against hiring anyone who can't learn from someone else or always has to be right or have the final word. Those characteristics won't work when operating as a member of a team. Each member must work together—equally—to achieve the overall solution, plan, budget, and buy in we are striving to accomplish. Learning isn't something that ends when we master a facet of our position. There is always room for improvement, whether we find a faster, more efficient way to perform a task, learn to better resolve issues between team members or between staff and clients, or we work on improving our own heart of service. If you hire someone who doesn't recognize that he or she could improve, you can't expect them to do so. Nor should you expect them to desire to serve with a spirit of excellence.

Affecting Change

Every business has its strengths and weaknesses. So does everyone who works there, from the CEO all the way up to the front line staff. Humility admits that things aren't always perfect, and there's always room for improvement—in yourself and in the company. Maybe one of our team members has noticed a flaw in the system that's affecting the atmosphere or the flow in the workplace. How does one go about bringing up what's in need of repair or start to affect change in the environment?

Relationship is at the heart of the spirit of hospitality, and that's where change begins. Everyone has a circle of influence in both their personal lives (immediate relationships such as spouses, children, parents, friends) and their social lives (co-workers, congregations, organizations). It's there we start to affect change.

First, we must recognize the things within us that need to change and be willing to work toward making those changes. Is there anything we're doing that is negatively affecting our performance? That's the best place to start, because we're the only ones we can change for sure. We also have the ability to influence those around us. Have you ever noticed that when you make a dramatic change in your life, whether it be losing weight, choosing to care more about others even when they come against you most times, or straightening out your financial mess that others begin commenting on the change they see? Has that ever turned into influencing them to make necessary changes in their own life? That's because when we toss a pebble into a pond, it has a ripple effect. The ripple starts with the stone—us. As we begin to impact others with our servanthood, they begin to impact those around them, and the influence expands.

Once we've started with ourselves, the next way to affect change is to start with those closest to us. Is there someone on our team that we can bring on board to begin to affect change in the workplace? Someone who may have a slightly different circle of influence than we do? Maybe it's the difference between a day shift and a night shift or the team we work on. Think about it. If one person can make one ripple effect, imagine what two can do. Teamwork only multiplies the effect.

After we've involved those closest to us, we need to start using our network. Every business has a chain of command. If we don't know the man or woman in charge, we probably know someone at our workplace who knows someone who does or who knows him or her themselves. There comes a point where if we've mentioned something to our leadership and we haven't seen any change within a reasonable amount of time, it becomes necessary to take it higher in the chain of command. This isn't the time to get pushy. It's a time for humility and accountability. When approaching someone up the chain of command or someone who knows that person, it's important to do so with an attitude of understanding, cooperation, and humility. Let them know what is happening, why there's need for change, and that you're willing to help in any way you can. It's important to avoid coming across as a know-it-all or to threaten to leave if we don't see the change effective immediately. That may stigmatize our future.

Once we've gone as far up the ladder as we can, it is important to consider whether the results are effective and improving the situation or if it may be time to find another place of employment that lines up with our values more than our current workplace. We also have to consider whether leaving will thwart the necessary change. If we quit, will it negatively affect an outcome that may be a month or three or twelve down the road? We need to be sure our ripple of influence has time to take effect before we walk out on potential change.

One final key to affecting change is to start small and allow things to grow organically. Don't try to force yourself into the bigger atmosphere. We're seeking success, not suffocation or crushing.

As leaders, we must allow team members to offer suggestions for change. These are the front-line servants. They deal with the guests and handle the workload every day. If something isn't functioning properly, chances are someone on our team will know what that is and have an idea of what could correct the issue. We should never doubt the intelligence, creativity, and capability of our team members. Their input and buy-in are critical for a long-term commitment to our company.

TAKEOUT:

▸ Change must begin with us.
▸ We're always learning, and we need to be open to the lessons being taught.
▸ Never be afraid of change, and never be afraid to mention when something should be changed.
▸ Change is good.

If you can't measure it, you can't manage it.
LARRY STUART HOSPITALITY

16

Return on Investing in the Spirit of Hospitality

ROI is simply dollars and cents. ROR (Return on Relationship) is the value (both perceived and real) that will accrue over time through connection, trust, loyalty, recommendations, and sharing.

- TED RUBIN

Whether we're running the Ritz Carlton or LaQuinta Inn & Suites, working at Ruth's Chris or Chick-fil-A, our ability or lack thereof to operate with the spirit of hospitality will drive our business higher or into the ground. Whether we're serving the well-off or the working man or woman, our genuine guest service needs to be exceptional, over the top. Obtaining the return guest and the client who will bring his friends back with him or shout her praises via Facebook and Twitter is the goal. The only way to achieve that goal is to weave the spirit of hospitality into every nook and cranny of our business relationships, from the sanitation engineer to the CEO.

Once the spirit of hospitality becomes part of a business's culture, it becomes part of the team's DNA. We live and breathe the spirit of hospitality, allowing us to connect with others, developing relationships with those we interact with. And once that happens, it's just a matter of time before we see the rewards of that delivery, which include but are certainly not limited to:

- ▸ Quality of life increases
- ▸ Relationships improve
- ▸ Advancement
- ▸ Increase in finances or Return on Hospitality

The spirit of hospitality has been proven to drive a cash flow that trumps the competition. If it doesn't put our competition out of business, it will at least drive our top line in our favor. Business valuation, ROI, and stakeholder equity are then lined up for an absolute win.

Where Do We Stack Up?

Did you know that 60 percent of new restaurants close or change ownership in the first year of business, while 80 percent fail within five years? These failures are due to a variety of reasons, including:

- ▸ Lack of knowledge, Inexperience, or Owner who doesn't work the restaurant
- ▸ Lack of financial reserves to pay team members and keep the lights on due to poor budgeting or overspending, not paying taxes, or overpaying staff
- ▸ Bad location
- ▸ Poor guest service
- ▸ Poor food quality[19]

These are just to name a few. If we own a restaurant or hotel, run an airline or cruise ship, or are active in any other hospitality-related business, it's important to know where we stack up. Knowing where we stand amongst the competition and with guests will help us remain in business and not be part of the 60-80 percent of failed ventures.

ROI is about Relationship

Most businesses today are focused on top-line sales, pricing strategies, ROI, fighting the internet, and more when they should be focused on building relationships, being kind, and creating positive and memorable experiences for their guests. If we were providing the spirit of hospitality on a consistent basis, rather than worrying about meeting a sales quota for the day, our ROI would naturally improve, because the guests would be buying our service and then referring their friends. The spirit of hospitality must become the standard operating procedure.

Every company or CEO creates their individual "guest service initiative." This is the process they wish to implement in order to improve their guest loyalty and bottom-line profit. In our company, we hire individuals who possess a spirit of hospitality and willingness to improve by using their talents to the best of their ability and being directed through our leadership. Then, we introduce our quality service standards through a robust training program.

Throughout this process, we introduce our team members to the spirit of hospitality and immerse them in the ingredients we've discussed throughout this book. Our ultimate goal, of course, is creating the ultimate guest experience, which leads to guest satisfaction.

Let's take a moment to look at why guests don't return, as it's important to recognize a problem in order to fix it. Of course, it's better to prevent the problem in the first place, but sometimes these issues are beyond our control. Here are a few reasons why companies lose their guest basis:

- ▸ 1% Die
- ▸ 3% Move Away
- ▸ 5% Are Influenced by Friends
- ▸ 9% Are Lured Away by the Competition
- ▸ 14% Are Dissatisfied with a Product or Service
- ▸ *68% Are Turned Away by an Attitude of Indifference on the Part of a Company Team Member*[20]

That last statistic says a lot. It says there are people working in more than fifty percent of our establishments who could care less about our guests—including management. In cases this drastic, ownership and leadership are absent. Too many times I've been called to assess a business operation and found the establishment's number one cause of its failure to be an absentee owner. Instead of leading his company's leadership team, he's sitting back and watching ball games or going on fishing expeditions and expects the business to deliver without an investment of his time. Our business is one of the toughest, and the word auto-pilot isn't in our vocabulary. We'd have a better chance at a return in a Las Vegas casino than we would working in the hospitality industry. Without guests, we have no business. Indifferent servants turn off guests. When leadership invests in their staff, the staff operate properly. It's key to our success, growth, and viability that we master guest service through the spirit of hospitality. Otherwise, we'll be going out of business sooner than we think.

Studies show that if a business can demonstrate superior service, it can increase sales in its market share. The most important aspect of guest service is the treatment of our guests. Do we approach them with kindness, sincerity, and gratitude for their business? Because we need to. They are our bread and butter. They are what makes us successful. And in order for our guests to make our business successful, our team members need to be professional and personable as they approach our guests and meet their needs.

When we respond to guests with kindness, understanding, recognition of their emotions and issues, quick response, consideration, and resolution, we are far more likely to receive kindness, trust, loyalty, and returning guests who will tell all their friends about the admirable service they received at our establishments. We need to come to a place where we can offer a smile, a word of encouragement, a listening ear, and maybe even a prayer when a client is having a challenging time. Our goal is satisfied when we attract repeat and new guests, and we should do all we can in order to achieve that. It's unacceptable to have any other result in our service-based industry.

Where Do We Stack Up Externally?

Consider the reasons you patronize a restaurant, hotel, or fly with a particular airline. Did you feel special when you came through the door? Did the staff welcome you by name? Did they remember the details of your prior experiences and offer an equivalent or greater experience the next time you did business with them? Consistency. Great value. Expedited service. These are the things that allow for our business to grow. People return to our establishments because we have extended the spirit of hospitality. If we want to find out more about our guests' opinions, there are a few things we can do which can allow for making necessary changes based on their answers.

1. **Comment Cards:** Keep them simple so guests don't feel like they're doing homework. Compile results. Let team members know when they've been praised—openly. Correct those who've had negative feedback—in private. All challenges on the comment card should be taken seriously and corrected immediately.
2. **Surveys:** Talk to your guests. Ask specific questions. How can we improve our service? What would make you come back?
3. **Web Apps:** These may cost a small fee, but apps like User Voice and Feedbackify provide you direct contact with guests you may not hear from otherwise. Tech-savvy people will be more likely to fill out these surveys than the comment card at our local restaurants and hotels.
4. **Focus Groups:** Call a group of guests, invite them to participate in a sample group where they can taste test new menu items or stay overnight in a new hotel if they are willing to provide feedback, and have them brainstorm with you on how you could improve your service delivery.

These are ways we can obtain that information directly from our business source. But there are other ways to find out what our guests are saying about their experiences with us, and these may even be more easily attainable, because people love to talk with other consumers. The internet is a treasure trove of feedback. With sites like TripAdvisor, we can easily access guest reviews of our establishments.

How Do We Stack Up Inside?

The other important factor in our measurements should be team member satisfaction. If our internal guests aren't satisfied in their work, their productivity will decrease, which in turn will affect external guest service, which will affect our bottom line. So, it's important to know where we stand in all of these critical areas.

The following are three ways we can track how we're doing with our team members:

1. **Track the productivity of our staff:** How are they performing? Are they meeting goals? Getting jobs completed effectively and efficiently? If we find any lack in any area of their performance, this is a sign they could use further training or redirection.

2. **Staff reviews:** These may be hard to get, but they're available. How does the staff feel about the organization they work for? This is an opportunity for leaders to find out how they stack up and if they may need to improve their own performance as a result. We should never allow our team members to feel intimidated, afraid to give honest feedback about their leaders or fellow team members. If something is noted, it's imperative as servant leaders that we address the issues and strive for all-around improvement. Anything less will allow for disunity to creep into our team, which will affect their performance and attitude toward our guests. And that's something none of us can afford.

3. **Employment Satisfaction Index:** Knowing this will give CEOs insight on the effectiveness of their business culture. Do our team members appreciate what we've offered them, whether it's tools for success, compensation, benefits, bonuses, or even the office coffee service and other such company perks? Are we living up to our

vision, mission, and beliefs? Do our team members enjoy working for us?

John Maxwell says that at 4:30, everyone is getting ready to leave work at 5:00. That final half hour of the day becomes a waste for the company. The team members aren't focused, and as a result, they're not accomplishing anything. It's a race out the door. People can't wait to get out of work.[21] Is that the type of place where you want to work or that you want your team members working? What can we do to adjust our business culture so the team members will want to work their full 8-hour day?

The goal is to lower our staff turnover rate. It can cost up to nine months' worth of a team member's salary to replace them. It's very important to know who is being turned over, which positions turn over more, and why. Is it the team member's performance? Their attitude? Or could it be ours in leadership? Have the team members been offered better employment opportunities elsewhere? All of these will play into turnover, and we will need to adjust accordingly if we're going to minimize this expense in order to improve our ROI.

Where we stack up inside our company all comes down to providing a sincere, transparent, engaging, and encouraging atmosphere for our internal guests—our team. Building a relationship with them builds trust and provides for a long-term tenure at our company.

How Do We Stack Up in the Industry?

If we're going to make a wave in our industry, we need to better understand our competitors and how we should best compete. Mostly, this is a numbers game. We run our monthly profit and loss statement to see our financial performance, noting any increases or decreases in our ROI. Once we've done that, we can start to look at our competition.

The first thing to do is set up a competitive set analysis. Identify what's in our immediate market that compares to our establishment. Look at the cars in their parking lot. Go inside during peak hours or seasons and count guests. Are we competing fairly from our marketing efforts, such as a third day on us or an airline upgrade?

The second way we can tell if we compete is by checking with sources such as JD Powers, Trip Advisor, industry journals, and relevant statistics. If our competition is publicly owned, their numbers will be posted. Do we have a benchmark rating? Have we won awards? These are all ways to gauge our place within market competition.

When we have a benchmark and know that our rating is a C- or a 65% or we are only making 1.3 million dollars, we have something to guide our choices over the next quarter, season, or year. If we're wise business leaders and hold ourselves accountable, we'll strive to implement changes that will allow us to improve that mark. How do we do that? The spirit of hospitality will showcase our brand by providing the competitive edge through our service execution. It's really that simple.

We can't track growth if we don't track our guest base or our numbers. When we do these things, we are better able to manage running the business and bringing our services up to guest expectations, which will then lead to the growth in our guest base and our ROI we'd love to have. It's only a win-win-win when we apply the principles of this book into our daily walk in life and in business in order to change culture back to the way it's supposed to be—treating one another with respect and serving one another selflessly.

TAKEOUT:

There are three areas we need to be aware of if we are going to increase our ROI:

1. Our external guests' satisfaction
2. Our internal guests' satisfaction
3. How we stack up in the industry against our competition

When we focus on treating one another with respect and serving one another selflessly, our ROI naturally increases. It's the ultimate way to create satisfied guests, who will bring new guests with them when they return.

Say thank you more often, and your life will be blessed.
LARRY STUART HOSPITALITY

17

Gratitude

Gratitude can transform common days into thanksgivings, turn routine jobs into joy, and change ordinary opportunities into blessings.
- WILLIAM ARTHUR WARD

Sometimes, as leaders, we're called to the front lines after our team has done beyond all they can do to provide a guest what they've asked for, including the upgraded suite, best view in the house, and the golf and spa package. Yet they still aren't satisfied. Or the airline passenger has called customer service to complain about an issue with their flight, and even after offering to fly them to the moon and back in first class, they are still disgruntled and expect everything for free. Maybe we've provided for a company holiday party but missed a few opportunities for a perfect delivery. In return, we offered a reasonable reduction on their invoice and upgraded their food, beverage, and audiovisual provisions. If the guest remains unforgiving in these situations, we may have to acknowledge to ourselves and our staff that they will never be satisfied and that we have to take the high road.

It's difficult to perform under the stress of never getting it right. It's also difficult to deal with ungrateful people. Day in and day out, we serve others. Sometimes, we receive a tip or a nod of the head. Sometimes we face the guest's wrath. Regardless, it's important that we maintain an attitude of gratitude in every situation we find ourselves in.

Thankfulness is one of many keys to a humble heart. Regardless of our circumstances, there is always something to be thankful for. It can be as simple as the breath in our lungs. We're alive today. We have another chance to get something right, to overcome a weakness. Someone took a moment and smiled when we needed a reason to do so ourselves. Maybe our team leader is being a downright jerk one day and our coworker, who witnessed his rampage, stopped by to give us a word of encouragement. As long as we draw breath, we have a reason to be grateful.

How do we walk in this attitude of gratitude when everything around us is seemingly falling apart? We make a choice. We choose not to let others' emotions and actions become personal and take us down their negative path. Instead, we choose the spirit of hospitality. Happiness is circumstantial. Joy comes from within. If you walk in joy, life's challenges bounce off you. No one can steal your joy. You have to give it away in order not to walk in it. So, the next time someone tries to suck the life out of you, whether it's your boss, a team member, or a guest, choose joy. Be thankful for the job that pays your bills and puts food on your table. Be thankful that your spouse loves you and hasn't left you like so many others. Be thankful that your child is still alive and is healthy, because someone out there has lost a son to a drug overdose or has children fighting a chronic or terminal illness and is running back and forth to the doctors' and the surgeons' offices on a daily basis.

We serve day in and day out. Sometimes the only reward is our paycheck at the end of the week. But if we can change our mentality and look at our job through the lens of being the one person who can make a true difference in our guests' lives, our entire perspective can change. We can offer an encouraging word, a helping hand, or a plate of food. And in doing so, we give someone else something to be thankful for that day.

Someone I admire and am extremely grateful for is Pierre Derosier. This enthusiastic man lives, breathes, and oozes the spirit of hospitality. He served as my banquet captain when I owned and operated the downtown

Orlando Embassy Suites food service operation. He performed at a level that not only exceeded our guests' expectations but went above and beyond any written training standard. His work ethic was solid, and he sincerely contributed daily to our team and our guests. When someone has the positive, can-do attitude that Pierre does, guests flock to the establishment. We had guests who would only return if Pierre was available to work with them. That's how effective an attitude of gratitude paired with a passion for our job and serving others can be. Are you a Pierre? How grateful are you for the guests you serve?

TAKEOUT:

When we recognize that life isn't about us, it becomes easier to be thankful when serving others.

Do you want a life of success, or do you want a life of purpose and significance?

LARRY STUART HOSPITALITY

Self-care and the Spirit of Hospitality

Never get so busy making a living that you forget to make a life.
- **DOLLY PARTON**

There was a fisherman who lived in a small village on the coast of Mexico. One afternoon, he pulled up to the dock with several large yellowfin tunas in his tiny boat. An American businessman noticed him and complimented the quality of his fish. "How long did it take you to catch them?"

"Only a short time."

"Why didn't you stay out longer and catch more?" the American inquired.

"I have enough to meet my family's immediate needs."

"But what do you do with the rest of your time?"

He replied that he slept late, fished a little, played with his children, took siestas, strolled with his wife into the village each evening and sipped wine and played guitar with his friends. He had a full and busy life.

The American couldn't understand why the Mexican fisherman wouldn't want to get a bigger boat, catch more fish, sell them directly to the processors, and eventually open his own cannery. He could then control the product, processing, and distribution. All he'd have to do is leave his small village in Mexico and move to Mexico City, Los Angeles, and eventually New York City, where he could run his entire empire.

When the Mexican asked how long that would take, the American told him fifteen to twenty years. And then, when the time was right, he could sell his company's stock to the public and become exceedingly rich.

"Then what would I do?" he asked.

The American told him he could retire and move to a small, coastal fishing village where he could enjoy all the things he was already doing.

The author of this story is unknown, but the story provides something powerful for us to think about. When is enough, enough? This industry can take a lot out of us if we don't take care of ourselves and our loved ones.

When I was building my career, it was normal to work 100 hours per week with just a few days off each year. Building businesses and leading them took time, and time was money. I was out the door by five in the morning, arriving at the hotel or restaurant by six, and not returning home until ten or later that night. I worked thirteen to fifteen hours most days for a year at a time while opening and operating new properties and working out all the kinks.

I realized that life was too short to have my epitaph read "I wish I spent more time at the operations office." Work can't be more important than family. Relationships are at the heart of the Spirit of Hospitality— they require consistent love and attention, and they should always come first.

Thankfully, the men and women who are leading today's corporations are beginning to recognize the importance of relationships and the need for rest and play. Values are refocusing on family and health. Millennials are seeking purpose in their positions. Corporations are including perks for their team members including extended maternity leaves for both fathers and mothers, whether they're giving birth or adopting. They're offering classes to improve team members' all-around health, whether they need further assistance with getting into shape physically, emotionally, or financially. Some are paying for time off to grieve the loss is of a loved one, friend, or pet. Others are also paying for team members to take time off to care for sick children or elderly parents. Other perks include on-site gyms, free or subsidized meals with healthy choices, and rooms for staff to relax in during breaks. On-site childcare is also cropping up.

We've realized we can't be sharp and on our game without the necessary rest. Getting away from the day-to-day grind allows our minds an opportunity to refresh our creative talents and energy levels, enabling us to be more productive when we return our focus to our work. Kimpton Hotels and Restaurants allows their general managers, executive chefs, and Home Office and regional crew members who are directors or higher to take one month of paid sabbatical leave for every seven years they've been in service to the company. The requirement is that they have to unplug from their jobs. They're not allowed to answer email or phone calls that are business-related while on sabbatical.[22] Princess Cruises Shore Side team members in Santa Clarita, California enjoy working nine-hour days with a full day off every two weeks so they can spend quality time with their families and take care of personal needs.[23] Or they can simply recharge.

It's important to remember that relationships are at the heart of all we do. If someone's relationships at home are strained, it will affect their performance at work. It's difficult to focus on the tasks at hand when you had an unresolved argument with your spouse before you left for your job. The weight of that will hang on all day. If we notice something is off with someone's attitude, we may want to pull them aside and make sure they aren't harboring the pain of issues at home or with another team member—or even us, their leaders. Would it really put a dent in the day if we enabled our team members to take an extra fifteen minutes at home to resolve an issue or to take the day of the board meeting off so they can attend to a sick child or attend a graduation? As long as there is transparent and honorable communication with their team leaders, allowing team members to focus on their key relationships first could mean a world of difference not only in their lives, but in our company's bottom line as well.

If our team members or we are feeling a bit overwhelmed, under productive, or just plain tired, it may be time for us to consider how much time we're putting in at the hotel, restaurant, airline, or cruise ship and whether we're overworking ourselves and our staff. A simple adjustment to our schedules may be all it takes to increase productivity, put smiles back on our faces, and improve our guest service delivery. Which leads to improving our bottom line.

TAKEOUT:

In order to have an all-around healthy lifestyle, keep the following points in mind when you're doing business:

- ▸ Life can't be all about work and no play.
- ▸ Our bodies naturally require rest.
- ▸ Relationships need to come first.

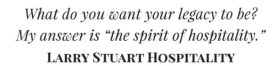

What do you want your legacy to be?
My answer is "the spirit of hospitality."
LARRY STUART HOSPITALITY

19

Leaving a Legacy of Hospitality

Carve your name on hearts, not tombstones. A legacy is etched into the minds of others and the stories they share about you.
- SHANNON L. ALDER

There was once a young boy who was walking along the beach when he came across an area where thousands of starfish had all washed ashore. He began picking them up, one at a time, and tossing them back into the ocean. An older man came along and laughed. He didn't see how throwing them back one at a time could possibly make a difference in their death toll. But the young man knew that he could make a difference, even if it was one starfish at a time. The moral of the story? If we all do our part, we'll make a difference. What could happen if multiple people were throwing one back at a time? The chances of survival—or turnaround—multiply substantially. What are you going to do to affect the necessary change? It only takes one person one committed act at a time...

What's Your Purpose?

If you ask any of my family members, they'll tell you I had an inborn gift of hospitality. Raised in an Italian family who was always in the kitchen, I learned Nana's (Mom's mom) recipes early in life. Grandma (Dad's mom) would cook 10-course meals, pack them in boxes, tie the boxes with sheets and twine, and bring it to wherever the family was. It was still hot when we devoured it. Mom and I canned tomatoes every year and made wine with my cousin, Ralph. And my Aunt Phyllis was another incredible cook. I was raised in the kitchen.

We are all born with gifts and talents, and at a typically young age, we start to dream about how we can use them to make our world a better place. I started my career in hospitality at a very young age, while on the road with my famous father, who worked in the entertainment industry. I learned a lot about the hotel and restaurant business as we travelled around the country. There wasn't much for a young boy to do at the hotels we stayed in, so I filled my time serving the staff, helping out in any way I could. That servant spirit remained deep within me as we celebrated holidays as a family, as I created meals in the kitchens with my grandmothers, and as I grew to be old enough to work in the light and sound booth at events where my father would be performing.

I loved serving others, but I also loved entertaining people and pursued a career in showbiz, following in my father's footsteps. I performed at high-end clubs, acted in commercials, and spent several years on the road as the opening singing act for Phyllis Diller.

But my father knew that the entertainment industry was unstable, and a person could be famous one day and not the next. In his wisdom, he convinced me to attend Cornell University's School of Hotel and Restaurant Administration. I had reservations about whether or not I was qualified, could succeed at that level of academia, or could even make it through school. How did I qualify to attend an Ivy League school? One of my father's many friends knew the right people, and he helped me get my foot in the door. Dad drove me to the campus and dropped me off at my dorm. "This is it. This is where you're going." It wasn't what I dreamed of doing at the time, but my father and mother understood the struggle of entertaining others. They wanted to be sure I had a backup plan for when my entertainment career no longer paid the bills or my spotlight burned out.

As Phyllis Diller had taught me while I was on the road with her, I found I had the four Ds—the Drive, Determination, Discipline, and Direction—necessary to excel at my education, and I successfully graduated from Cornell. But, after a short stint in the hospitality industry, I found myself back in the entertainment business, because that's what I thought I wanted to do. I loved the spotlight, and I loved making others laugh. However, no matter how hard I tried, I couldn't find fulfillment there. My heart was to serve others. Discovering my true identity would lead to my true purpose. It was then that I truly succeeded and went on to have an incredible career in hospitality. I learned that if I worked in a field that I loved and did so with passion, I never had to work again. My career was my passion.

Often, it's in hindsight that we can see our steps ordered along the path of life. It takes years of experiences and gaining understanding, knowledge, and wisdom before we can look back and see where circumstances and moments in time intersected and developed us into the individuals we've become today—whether we're successful or we fail. As you think back, can you find a few points in your timeline of life when things seemed to fall into place for that dream to become a reality? Maybe you met someone who knew someone in your field. Maybe you learned a skill you would need to do that job. Maybe someone blessed you with a gift that could help make your dream a reality. These are indicators that we are moving in a direction in life that we were meant to move in. We're on the right path.

Consider where you've come from and where you are today. Do you see yourself as a success? Or do you have a deep longing to be something more or to do something different? If you aren't satisfied with who you are or where you are today, maybe it's time for a change. Don't stay in that place. Time is short. Why spend your life doing something you get no joy from doing or have no passion for? That's not living.

Why is this important in a book about the spirit of hospitality and how to infuse that spirit into our business in order to make it successful? Because if we or our team members aren't passionate about working in the hospitality industry—if we haven't dreamed of owning a restaurant or partnering with someone and owning a hotel—our guests will notice. Our intentions, performance, and results will always reveal the truth about our heart for service. We need to be passionate about serving others if we're to succeed in hospitality.

Life Isn't All About Me

Transitioning from a career in entertainment, where the spotlight was always on Larry, into a career in hospitality, where life was all about serving others, took some significant adjustments. Figuring out that life isn't all about me didn't happen overnight, or even in one instance. For me, it was a series of events throughout my adulthood that revealed I wasn't "all that and a bag of chips" and that others depended on me and my services. Transitioning from show business into the hospitality industry brought many lessons about selflessness with it.

Shortly after he shipped me off to Cornell, my father left my mother. Recognizing a need, I stepped up to the plate and began to serve those closest to me—Mom and my sister, Andi. When I went through a divorce and remarried later, I recognized I needed to put others before my own desires. What I learned through all of these life-changing events is that when we are willing to lay our lives down for our friends and family— even strangers—the rewards are more than we can count. The greatest of these is having the ability to leave a legacy. Making millions and being the CEO of a large company is not the win when it all stays behind. Building our treasure with the greater purpose of leaving a legacy will bring more self-worth, integral character, and confidence than money ever will.

Leaving a Legacy

We are members of a larger body who are all working together toward a common goal—living an abundant life while operating in love toward one another. Now, abundance isn't always "stuff" oriented. Riches are far more than monetary. The more important inheritance is one of serving others with integrity, encouragement, accountability, kindness, generosity, and humility in team unity. And when we operate in these ingredients, others are blessed. Which is a far greater legacy than "stuff."

We can't take money and stuff with us when we die. There isn't going to be a U-Haul attached to our hearse. We don't go to funerals and hear about how much money is left in the deceased's bank account. We go to hear the stories about who the person was, what he or she did for us—the difference they made in our lives—and what we loved about them. That's the true treasure in life. Love. Service. And the inheritance of something far greater than gold. It's character. What inheritance are we leaving for the next generation? How are we living our dash—the time between our birth and our death? What will everyone we knew say about us when we pass away? Personally, I would like to know I've left a legacy of serving those I've known with love and generosity. I'd like to know I've passed my spirit of hospitality on to the generations behind me so they, too, can bless others with their service.

Live a Generational Life

We should take every opportunity to pass on the values we hold close to our heart. Whether we're at home, at our workplace, or in a social environment, generational living should be at the forefront of our minds. Finding someone to mentor should be a priority. Consider who mentored you or made an impact in your life. Who are your heroes? What did that person or those people do to encourage you to strive to be the best person you could be or to do something with excellence? How can you do the same for someone else? The greatest reward is to give of yourself for a colleague or a friend. There is no better return on your investment than this action.

My Uncle, Lou Marsilia, invested in me when I was young. During the summer months, I worked in his tool and die shop in Cambridge, Massachusetts. It was a dirty job where I learned about responsibility and accountability. When we weren't working, he would cook with me, sharing family values and teaching me about life. He mentored me while Dad was on the road. At a time when I needed a father's attention, Uncle

Lou stepped up and took me under his wing. He and Auntie Lil freely gave of themselves and impacted my life in a way I would never forget. There is no value we can place on the spirit of hospitality when it is truly given from the heart.

It's important to pass on what we know, because in today's world, there is so much lacking. People don't understand or refuse to acknowledge how to treat one another with kindness and respect, have a conversation with differing viewpoints and not turn it into a hate fest, or simply love on one another. Our kids don't respect authority and walk around with entitlement attitudes. Unfortunately, they probably get it from their role models—us. Which means that we are the ones lacking a spirit of hospitality. And we have work to do to change that. If we're going to improve our businesses and our bottom lines, we need to improve our spirit of hospitality and hold those we pass it on to accountable. We need to get back to sincerely caring about our neighbor and treating each other the way we would like others to treat us. We need to follow the golden rule. If we're the few who recognize the need for that, we need to be diligent to pass that on to our family members, co-workers, and even our leaders. We need to be an example not only to the people who work for us, but also to the people we work for. Again, we need to treat others the way we want to be treated, put our best foot forward, and serve with a spirit of excellence.

People won't care how much we know until they know how much we care. The best way to demonstrate that we care is to be a living example of the spirit of hospitality. Talk with coworkers. Ask them how they're doing and if there's anything you can do to help. Bless someone with a kind word of encouragement or small token of your appreciation. This even applies to those who you work *for*. When we understand and respect authority, we recognize that there is always someone overseeing us, just as we are overseeing others. We're always accountable to someone. It's not brown-nosing to honestly care for someone, even our bosses. Once we've developed trust and established a relationship, it's much easier to teach a principle or skill. Everyone can learn something from someone else, and it's never too late to learn something new. Learning should be a lifetime endeavor.

Ron Brennan accepted an offer to be vice president of a startup airline, Kiwi Airlines, and he brought me in to provide customer service training for the entire company. As a mentor, Ron provided me the opportunity to succeed in life by offering me multiple choices and allowing me to figure out the solutions myself. He would advise without placing his own opinions on what I should or shouldn't do. He offered wisdom, experience, and a love of his fellow man that exceeded his years. Ron remains a man who operates in the spirit of hospitality today. He not only taught me, he lived it himself. And through time, his testimony as a mentor stood true. He has passed his knowledge on to multiple individuals, myself included.

Sometimes we miss the blessing of having someone else pouring into us. It's not that we don't notice that they've served us. It's that we aren't aware of the cost of what they've done for us. When we recognize the gift we've been given, it's natural to want to thank the person who gave it, but it's also natural to want to give back. Here are a few ways to do so:

1. **Honor the person who gave the gift.** Can you write a thank you note or send an email? Can you speak well of them to someone else who may know them or may not know them? If the person is deceased, is there a charity they supported that you can make a donation to?

2. **Pay it forward.** Consider the person who mentored you or someone who taught you something invaluable. Is there anyone you know who could use the same information? Could you pour yourself into them for a season?

3. **Donate your time to serve someone else.** I've often heard counselors encourage people who are focused on themselves to serve someone else with no expectation of receiving something in return. This is a great way to get past a spirit of entitlement.

Leaders are like eagles—they don't flock. You find them one at a time. Look at your current team. Who among them is a natural leader? Spend some extra time getting to know him or her this week and consider serving them until they're ready to advance into a leadership position. Put them on your shoulders and then watch them take off and fly!

My hope is that maybe now God can use me on the stage once again, this time as a humble speaker who can teach others how to walk in a spirit of hospitality, putting others before themselves.

TAKEOUT:

Consider the following questions, and journal your answers if you'd like:

1. Is there a mentor who means the world to you? What can you do to thank him or her for serving you with a spirit of hospitality?
2. Do you know someone who you could pour into? What can you do right now to encourage them in their goals?
3. What personal legacy would you like to leave? What's one thing you can do today toward leaving that legacy?

Imagine - Believe - Achieve
LARRY STUART HOSPITALITY

20

Lucio Arancibia, The Epitome of the Spirit of Hospitality

We believe in doing work that we love and, in choosing that,
nudging others toward doing what they love.
And of all the heroic pursuits large or small, we believe there
may be none greater than a life well loved.
- CHIP AND JOANNA GAINES *FROM THE MAGNOLIA MANIFESTO*

A few years ago, Lucio Arancibia was asked to address the culinary students at the College of Southern Nevada. He would hopefully motivate them to a point determine if they were on the right career path. Lucio started his speech by asking, "Who wants to be a Chef?" The entire room raised their hand. A few second later, he asked, "Who wants to be a cook?" The entire room was silent. You see, it takes a tremendous sacrifice to be successful. It requires commitment, determination, and love for what we do. And Lucio is a shining example of success.

Lucio's passion for food began at a young age. His mother required all six of her children to help make dinner, so he or one of his five siblings would clean something while another would peel potatoes. It was at home where he learned to work together with others as a team. And it's his mother who inspired him to pursue his passions.

In the summer of 1976, Lucio made the decision to emigrate to a country far away, where they didn't speak his language and he wouldn't be able to understand what anyone was saying to him. With a 40-dollar loan from his uncle in his pocket, he left Argentina and embarked on a journey to America, not knowing if he would ever see his family and dear friends again.

With his uncle's loan, he was able to secure a plane ticket to Mexico. Three days later, he met a Coyote—a tour guide—who told him it would only take two hours to reach the border. He bought himself a can of 7-UP and set out. The 7-UP only lasted half an hour, but he trekked the Mexican dessert for nine hours in the middle of the summer, with temperatures over 115 degrees. Once he got to the United States, he went to Canada and then legally returned to the US to become a citizen. This began Lucio's lifelong journey of serving the spirit of hospitality.

Lucio's story would take him to New Jersey, where he joined his sister. She had married an American and become the first of his family members to become a United States citizen. He served at various hotels as a chef in New York, Kansas, and Tennessee before arriving in Las Vegas, Nevada. After a brief season at the old MGM, he spent a tenure serving as executive chef at Excalibur. For Lucio, Excalibur was a great training ground. He discovered that people who were committed to their passion for the hospitality industry and had a vision for it found Excalibur— and Vegas—a great place to work. The volume of business in Vegas was incredible, unlike anywhere else he'd experienced. For him, work meant making sure the menus worked in eleven restaurants, keeping them in conjunction with Excalibur's medieval theme.

During this time, Lucio was recognized for his distinction for cuisine. While in Nevada, the American Culinary Federation named him Las Vegas' top chef in 1995. Because of his compassion for others, he raised $300,000 for the Ronald McDonald House the year he was honored. But he didn't only serve the external customers. He also served his internal customers. Lucio developed his own employee-relations handbook, based upon interaction with those he served alongside. His fusion of real-life stories and conversational techniques connect with his staff at an intimate, intense, and individual level. His advice rings true to the spirit of hospitality. "You should engage your employees daily, make them involved. When there is a lack of engagement, people feel that they don't exist. You want to focus on the positive. We all want recognition; it's more important than money. Recognize a person in front of 10 people and it works wonders.

A distinguished chef, Lucio left Las Vegas in 2003. It was then he had the honor of preparing a pastry dish for Vice President Cheney at the White House, making him a Guest Director/Chef at the White House. "You whip up something special, and people go 'wow'. You can barely describe that feeling." Since then, he's been many places. Lucio has over 30 years of experience in the hospitality industry in all facets of food and beverage operations and has held senior positions with Mandalay Resort Group, Bally's Grand Resort, The Hermitage Hotel and the New York Hilton.

Traveling has taught Lucio a lot about diversity. It's important to him to help people become better in their life, to eliminate barriers that would prevent them from being self-motivated. How we choose to experience accountability and responsibility is a moment-to-moment personal choice and has nothing to do with title, tenure, or position. With a visionary force behind his leadership gift, he applies groundbreaking discoveries about personal responsibility and performance to support future leaders who are intent on rapidly building highly reliable, agile, sustainable, and accelerating teams and cultures. He's a dynamic individual that shares best practices for collaborating under competitive conditions. Lucio has mastered responsibility within organizations and shares how high-performing individuals, teams, and business cultures influence responsibility to create impact. The commitment, his work, and his passion is the first how-to approach for taking and teaching personal responsibility. These rich discoveries are changing how the staff engages, how leaders lead, how teams get built, and how trainers teach and inspire personal responsibility. He has inspired and created sustainable changes within organizations.

Behind it all, Lucio is convinced that simplicity will improved the life of hard working chefs of all walk of life. He is always inspired and guided by the same obsessive drive and belief, that everything should be simple. "I hope that I made a positive impact on all those that I came in contact during my priceless culinary journey. I am grateful for those that provided the much-needed support that helped me reach the next step.

Today Lucio serves as the Director of Food and Beverages at The Sheraton Getaway at LAX, where he enjoys sunny Los Angeles. He reunited with his family when his parents moved to the US later in the 1980s. It was their dream come true, and they lived a beautiful life close to the son they were proud of until their deceases over the last decade.

THE 7 KEY INGREDIENTS

FOR THE SPIRIT OF HOSPITALITY

1. **Team Unity:** It's important for servant leaders to remember there is no "I" in team and come alongside their team members to serve both the internal and external guests. When internal guests trust their leaders, external guests are treated well.

2. **Encouragement:** Don't hold back on encouraging your team members. This is not an area in which to be stingy. Everyone loves encouragement. Figure out how your team members each receives encouragement best and be sure to use that method to demonstrate your appreciation for them and their hard work.

3. **Accountability:** As servant leaders, we must be willing to admit our mistakes. Doing so builds trust with both our internal and external guests. Trust leads to loyalty.

4. **Generosity:** Giving must come from a heart of service. When it does, there is more joy in that than there ever could be in earning a paycheck.

5. **Kindness:** A kind act or word has the power to make someone feel great. The value of kindness speaks the truth about a person's self-worth. When we act in kindness, the recipient is made to feel exceptional, important, and special. That is something we don't soon forget. And that is something the guest who enters your

establishment needs to feel as soon as they step foot through the door until the moment they leave.

6. **Humility:** Change must begin with us. We're always learning, and we need to be open to the lessons being taught. Never be afraid of change, and never be afraid to mention when something should be changed. Change is good.

7. **Gratitude:** When we recognize that life isn't about us, it becomes easier to be thankful when serving others.

ACKNOWLEDGEMENTS

First and foremost, this journey would not have been possible without the blessing of my Lord and Savior Jesus Christ.

I will always be humbly grateful to all those who have not been personally mentioned—there are just too many to thank—who have built me up with encouragement, wisdom, discipline, guidance, and love through my life journey in the "Spirit of Hospitality."

I want to sincerely thank my precious family, who have provided a strong foundation of discipline, integrity, and honor. They taught me early on that life was all about attitude and service, which kept me grounded and humble.

Mom and Dad—Esther Stuart and Enzo Stuarti

My Grandmothers—Ida Mesce and Maria Cicetti

My Second Mom—Aunt Phyllis Ilaria

My Best Friend and Sister—Andrea Leib and my Brother—Don Leib

My Second Families—Ricciani, Brennan, Marsilia, and Schepis

My Cousins—Ralph, Terry, Michael, and Michele

To my pastors, I thank you for your leadership, friendship, and encouragement. You have spiritually lifted me up through the years and always pointed me in the right direction, which confirms that God's plan works much better than mine. Thank you, Herkie Walls, David Uth, and Howard Edington.

To all of my Cornell University friends and colleagues, thanks for taking me under your wings and mentoring me on a journey through the hospitality industry:

Dr. Harry Seaburg, Dean Robert Beck, and Dean Michael Johnson.

Professors Donal Dermody, Peter Rainsford, Jerry Wanderstock, and Vance Christian.

Colleagues Peter Yesawich, Steve Weisz, Bill Fisher, John Berndt, Roberto Wirth, John Mariani, Drew Nieporent, Richard Holtzman, Bill Nassikas, Mike Green, and Tom Cleary.

To all my hospitality heroes and friends that I've had the pleasure to know and serve beside over the years, I can't thank you enough for all that you gave. Phil Pistilli, Bodo Von Alvensleben, Harris Rosen, Octavio Gomez, Rhonda Rhodes, John Griswold, John Labruzzo, Eric Rosenbaum, Danny Colombo, Jim Nagy, Bob Reppin, Mike Welly, Bill Rizzuto, Lucio Arancibia, Alan Villaverde, Mike Sansbury, Ferdinand Metz, Adnan Bizri, Susan Heller, Chefs Jack & Brian, and Peter George.

We moved to the great state of South Carolina, home of southern hospitality. It was there where fate and destiny met and delivered a world-class support team through my mentor and book coach. Thanks for all your support and guidance, Edie Melson and Alycia Morales.

Thanks to my distinguished friends Eric Reinhardt, Phyllis Diller, Rob Shapiro, Dan Needham, and Larry Freda, who provided wisdom and direction through the years.

My desire is to leave this legacy to be passed on through our children and grandchildren to those whom they touch:

Daughters—Raquel Stuart, Kayla Ramey Miner, and Courtney Ramey.

Son—Lance Ramey, who passed prior to this book being published.

Granddaughters—Kimber Ramey and Kamdyn Miner.

ABOUT THE AUTHOR

With 40+ years of experience in hospitality leadership with a focus on hotel, restaurant, airline operations, genuine guest service delivery systems, and marketing-sales strategies, Larry Stuart is the CEO and president of LS Hospitality. Larry holds a Bachelor of Science degree from Cornell University School of Hotel Administration and has positively impacted his teams and brands that include the Walt Disney World Dolphin, NASCAR Café, MotorCity Casino Hotel, Hilton Worldwide, Loews Hotels at Universal Orlando Resort, and Southwest Airlines.

Larry has contributed as a hospitality expert for FOX News, board member for the Florida Restaurant & Lodging Association, and has presided as president of the Cornell Hotel Society Florida for the past 10 years. He has also contributed as adjunct professor for Valencia College Orlando, and taught Cornell Hotel School course in Orlando, providing instruction on entrepreneurial business innovation, guest service delivery processes, and hospitality management.

Larry and his wife make their home in South Carolina. He is a dedicated family man who enjoys spending time with his wife, their three children and two grandchildren.

ENDNOTES

1. Haydn Shaw with Ginger Kolbaba, *Generational IQ* (Illinois: Tyndale House Publishers, Inc., 2015).
2. "Texas Roadhouse," Great Place to Work, accessed August 19, 2017, https://reviews.greatplacetowork.com/texas-roadhouse.
3. "Truett Cathy Biography," Chick-fil-A, accessed October 19, 2017, http://www.truettcathy.com/TruettCathyBiorgraphy.pdf.
4. "Benchmarks by Company, Limited Service Restaurants," ACSI American Customer Satisfaction Index, accessed August 18, 2017, http://theacsi.org/index.php?option=com_content&view=article&id=149&catid=&itemid=214&i+Limited-Service-Restaurants.
5. "Southwest Reroutes Flight for Woman to See Comatose Son," Fox News, May 27, 2015, http://www.foxnews.com/travel/2015/05/27/soutwest-reroutes-flight-for-woman-to-see-comatose-son.html.
6. Definition of Organizational Culture, Web Finance, Inc., 2018, http://www.businessdictionary.com/definition/organizational-culture.html.
7. Andrew Hill with John Wooden, *Be Quick –But Don't Hurry: Finding Success in the Teachings of a Lifetime*, 1st ed. (New York: Simon & Schuster, 2001).
8. Haydn Shaw with Ginger Kolbaba, *Generational IQ* (Illinois: Tyndale House Publishers, Inc., 2015).
9. "Ritz Carlton's *Gold Standard* Service," Ellis, accessed October 19, 2017, https://www.epmsonline.com/wp-content/uploads/2011/09/articles/RitzCarltonGoldStandardService.pdf.

10. T. Scott Gross, *Positively Outrageous Service*, 3rd ed. (New York: Allworth Press, 2016).

11. "Hyatt Hotels Corporation," Great Place to Work, accessed August 19, 2017, http://reviews.greatplacetowork.com/hyatt-hotels-corporation.

12. "7 Ways to Keep Employees Happy," Harvey Deutschendorf, Fast Company, January 17, 2014, https://www.fastcompany.com/3024949/7-ways-to-keep-employees-happy.

13. "Marriott International, Inc.," Great Place to Work, accessed August 19, 2017, http://reviews.greatplacetowork.com/marriott-international.

14. "At Disney, Everyone Picks Up Trash!," Jeff Kober, Mouse Planet, August 30, 2017, https://www.mouseplanet.com/6971/At_Disney_Everyone_Picks_Up_Trash.

15. "Texas Roadhouse," Great Place to Work, accessed August 19, 2017, https://reviews.greatplacetowork.com/texas-roadhouse.

16. Gary Chapman, *The Five Love Languages: How to Express Heartfelt Commitment to Your Mate* (Chicago: Northfield Publishing, 1995).

17. Steven R. Covey, *The 7 Habits of Highly Effective People*, 1st Fireside ed. (New York: Simon & Schuster, Inc., 1990), 236.

18. Ted Dekker, *The Forgotten Way* (Outlaw Studios, 2015), 198.

19. "Food Network Chef Robert Irvine Shares The Top 5 Reasons Restaurants Fail," Richard Feloni, Business Insider, February 25, 2014, http://www.businessinsider.com/why-restaurants-fail-so-often-2014-2.

20. "Why Companies Lose Customers," Jim Heilborn, INDEAL, February 13, 2017, http://www.indeal.org/single-post/2017/02/13/Why-Companies-Lose-Customers.

21. John C. Maxwell, *The 5 Levels of Leadership: Proven Steps to Maximize Your Potential* (New York: Center Street, 2011).

22. "Kimpton Hotels and Restaurants," Great Places to Work, accessed August 19, 2017, http://reviews.greatplacetowork.com/kimpton-hotels-restaurants.

23. "Princess Cruise Lines," Great Place to Work, accessed August 19, 2017, http://reviews.greatplacetowork.com/princess-cruises

Morgan James
Speakers Group

We connect Morgan James published authors with live and online events and audiences who will benefit from their expertise.

Printed in the USA
CPSIA information can be obtained
at www.ICGtesting.com
JSHW022328140824
68134JS00019B/1357